Wisdom *of the* Path

ALSO BY YASMINE CHEYENNE

The Sugar Jar

Wisdom
of the
Path

The Beautiful and Bumpy Ride to
Healing and Trusting Our Inner Guide

YASMINE
CHEYENNE

HarperOne
An Imprint of HarperCollinsPublishers

WISDOM OF THE PATH. Copyright © 2024 by Yasmine Cheyenne. All rights reserved. Printed in the United States of America. No part of this book may be used or reproduced in any manner whatsoever without written permission except in the case of brief quotations embodied in critical articles and reviews. For information, address HarperCollins Publishers, 195 Broadway, New York, NY 10007.

HarperCollins books may be purchased for educational, business, or sales promotional use. For information, please email the Special Markets Department at SPsales@harpercollins.com.

FIRST EDITION

DESIGNED BY BONNI LEON-BERMAN

Library of Congress Cataloging-in-Publication Data has been applied for.

ISBN 978-0-06-331500-6

24 25 26 27 28 LBC 5 4 3 2 1

To all who decide to take brave step after brave step on the journey of life. Continuing your path through triumphs of success and through tumultuous lows. Here's to the gained wisdom. Here's to hope. And here's to you.

And to my daughters, let my stories be a reminder that no matter how tough life gets, if we remember our humanness, we're in the kindest and most powerful position we could ever be in.

CONTENTS

Part 1

WHERE

YOU'VE

BEEN

1

THE STROLL OF A
LIFETIME:
A COURAGEOUS WALK

I was on my way home from work on a brisk fall evening, and as usual I was speed-walking from the Red Line train station, which was a few blocks away from my apartment. Every day after work I took the train home, about a thirty-minute commute, not bad for DC. But when I got home, I'd have to change with the speed of Wonder Woman before hopping in my car to pick up my then three-year-old daughter from preschool. Each day I had the same anxiety, because depending on traffic it could be a twenty-minute or forty-five-minute drive, and if it was the latter, I would be late and be assessed another fee. And I didn't need any more late fees.

I think about this moment in my life often, to the point where I can still see exactly how the sun was setting that evening. I can even see some of the cars and faces when I think back, even though it was over ten years ago. Some moments live in our minds temporarily, nonchalantly written in pencil on a Post-it and placed with the type of carelessness where you know it will eventually be forgotten. And others are carved in stone and nailed in place, where we couldn't forget the memory even if we wanted to. Those nailed-in moments help us construct a map of our lives, a blueprint, that represents our life experiences, major and minor, and ultimately inform our decisions. These impactful core moments are weaved together intricately, intertwining our wisdom, experience, and memories. The slightest smell, song, or question can evoke emotions and thoughts that act like coordinates, bringing us right back to that moment in time, and energetically allowing us to be a cartographer of our reality. We can see where we've been, we can witness where we are, and we can manifest where we want to go. I've noticed that not every moment is plotted on the map equally. Some moments come and go like the wind; we can feel their presence but we don't keep a record of their visits.

And other moments command our full attention, changing who we are and shifting how we see the world. Those latter moments are almost always plotted on our maps. And this situation was one of them.

A few days before this evening, I'd fed my daughter her full dinner while I ate a peanut-butter-and-four-crackers snack pouch. That snack was all I could afford at the time. I remember standing in my kitchen, emotionally but thankfully eating my snack for dinner while watching my daughter have her meal with the biggest smile on her face. I was so grateful that she was young enough to have no idea about my struggles in that moment. I was drowning in bills. I'd just moved into my own place post-separation, and it was more difficult than I was expecting. I was working constantly because I was afraid to lose my job. I also needed the overtime to help pay for all the late fees and necessities. I was even late on my rent a time or two, which was terrifying. I'd be up in bed most nights, with the stress of my circumstances fueling me like caffeine, ruminating over what I was going to do. I was overwhelmed and scared.

I kept my daughter in the same school she was in before my split, even though it was far from my new home, with the hope that having the same friends and teachers would help minimize the changes happening in her life. But the commute was rough. I wouldn't get home with her until about 7:30 each night, even though I'd leave work at 4:30 in the afternoon. When we finally arrived home, I'd slowly take her out of her car seat and carry her warm sleeping body upstairs. I'd wake her up for dinner and bath time and then it was time for bed so we could do it all again in the morning.

But on this brisk walk home, I was praying that I wouldn't have to make do with peanut butter and four crackers for dinner again. I was hungry, I was tired, and I needed help. I'd gone and tried to get resources, but was told that I made too much money to get support. Even if I wasn't ready to share that I needed help out loud with the people I knew, the energy of needing a miracle was dripping off me like ice cream in a cone on a hot summer day. I was falling apart.

The walk from the train station to my apartment went through a shopping center. I'd usually walk on the sidewalk, but today, I was cutting through the parking lot because I was rushing. As I walked through the cars of people filling their trunks with groceries, I remembered hoping to have that experience too, and soon. I wanted to have the freedom to fill my car with the groceries we needed. I didn't want to be so strapped for cash. And then I looked down at my feet and saw it.

When we're growing up, we often proclaim that we will never go through anything that we've declared as a flaw or mistake in our own upbringing. "I will do it *right*," we innocently affirm. It's only after we've spent some time with adulthood, and learned its true chaotic personality, that we realize what we're *really* dealing with. That perhaps this grown-up life isn't as easy as it seemed. It's why we encourage children to "enjoy being young" and to "not grow up too fast" because we know that as you gain autonomy in adulthood you also meet difficulties. What helps ground us in moments of uncertainty is the reminder that we've survived so much. That we have thrived despite all that we've seen and endured. And we can trade in our naive declarations of "getting it right" and instead plant our two feet on the ground and set off on our path with the wisdom we have guiding us along.

Whether you're revisiting old territory or starting something new, the guideposts throughout this book serve as a reminder that you're moving onward, even when the terrain is rough. These four guideposts are not a checklist. I wish I could tell you one existed, but I haven't found it. Instead, these guideposts chaperone us as we walk along. They don't give you the answers, but you can find your answers as you move through them. When viewing a map, you'll notice there are plenty of directions and places you can go, but only you know where you want to land. Society encourages us to find answers in "things." In success, in relationships, and in achievement.

But our wisdom is in the very vessel we've had since the day we were formed. It's within us.

In the story I share here, I was learning to have empathy for my parents, I was learning how to be vulnerable enough to let others in, and so much more, from what on the surface looked like just a story about being strapped for cash. For you, perhaps you're traversing the past, living in the shadow of childhood traumas as you parent your own children. Maybe you're in the thick of it—a divorce, an aging parent, a stagnant professional life that you know you can't keep living. Or are you planning for the future, contemplating what life will look like when you're able to make space for better, healthier routines?

I hope as you remember your stories while reading mine, you're invited to have more patience with yourself when you struggle. I hope it invites you to repair your relationship with yourself through forgiveness. Through this, we learn to love ourselves enough to show up and love others. We allow them to love us. We make space for community. We build connection. We invite others to walk with us instead of solo journeying for the rest of our lives.

Each transformative moment we experience stands tall as a monument within us, linking memories like strings of pearls, holding these enchanting moments of our life together. Laying pavers that await our steps.

BASE CAMP

Base camp is where we all start our paths, and where we gather the tools we'll need to get us to the other side of our journeys. We ask ourselves, *Have I been on this path before? What can I bring with me this time that, from experience, I know will help me? Is there anyone who can help reflect what I'm unable to fully see? How did this journey begin? Was I initiated on this path by life? Or did I come here on my own, ready to start again? What do I need to safely land where I want to go? Am I also prepared to land wherever life takes me?*

Have you ever thought you were ready to make a life-changing decision, when really you couldn't because you hadn't admitted the full stinking hard-to-hear truth of where you were? I know I've been there. I was right there in that parking lot. I felt ashamed. And shame is why we lie to ourselves in the first place. It's an unintentional way to keep ourselves from being hurt when we're already maimed. It's why I wasn't ready to tell anyone how much I was suffering. I wasn't ready to hear the "I told you so" statements. I wasn't ready to be judged. Mostly by myself.

I'm sure you've been there with situations in your life. Where you are walking on a rocky path and hoping that any moment now, you'll reach solid ground. A ground so solid that you could blindly put one foot in front of the other without having to fear that any misstep could take you right down.

When I was growing up, I watched a lot of horror films, and in them the character that's about to be attacked is usually doing some very mundane task, like making popcorn or taking a shower. They're quietly absorbed in living their lives and making their evening plans, and they have no idea what's coming for them. But we do. As the viewer on the outside, we can see that while they're blissfully getting ready for a night of relaxation, there's a psycho waiting outside their window. And even though we know there's about to be a moment of shock, when they finally realize they're in the fight of their lives, we're still frightened and scream when the character comes face-to-face with the fact that this isn't going to be the cozy night in they planned. Ah, so they think they can run to the phone and call for help? Nope, said psycho already thought of that, and their line is disconnected. Everything feels like it's closing in on them. They're caught completely off guard, and they're panicked.

This is how life can feel sometimes. Every time you try to turn a corner and do something different, a new shock is there waiting. We use the language that we feel "boxed in" for this very reason. And though this claustrophobic experience of feeling stuck is temporary, when you're in the middle of it, it feels like there's no escape or relief.

The quiet and cozy life that I thought I'd be able to build as a single mom was a horror film during this time. And for you, who have probably had a moment or two where your life reflected a nightmare, I can assure you that this sense of unpredictability is what base camp feels like for most during tough times. Maybe you're at a place on your journey where you feel out of options. You might even feel lost. For me, I knew I was beyond penny-pinching, but we can lie to ourselves for a long time. I wasn't ready to admit how deep in the mud I'd fallen. I thought I could dig myself out because I was pretending it was a puddle rather than admitting it was the abyss. We lie to ourselves, hoping that if we ignore the storm in front of us it won't damage us as it moves by. But it's acknowledging the storm that frees us. Until we have that moment of awareness, the moment where we know we must face the facts, we can't begin to move forward on our journey again. We can't save ourselves until we have that moment of honesty. We won't even allow other people in to help us until we have that moment of honesty. We can't be the hero in our own story without that moment of reckoning.

At base camp, you get to ask yourself questions like:

What would I tell someone who was going through this?

Remember, the advice we'd give to someone we love is often the very words we need to hear ourselves.

What do I need from the people who I know would love to support me, if they knew I needed them?

This question brings attention to two very important things. 1) Are people aware that you need help? You can't receive what you need if you don't speak up. 2) Are you asking the people who you know would love to support you? Release the urge to force people to do what you need because you think "they're my parent, sister, friend, or cousin, so they should want to do this for me." On journeys like these, it becomes clear who is there for you, no matter what title or role they hold in your life. Hold the people who show up closely and keep going.

How can I lean into courage and create the village that I yearn for?

There's a lot of discussion about building villages and not enough discussion about how hard it is. And yet we need them. These are the people who will hold us when times get hard. Ask yourself, Do I have the time, space, and energy to create the community I'm craving? Strong friendships are a lifeline. Don't worry, we'll talk about this more throughout the book.

INTENT

Intent is where we purposefully plot our path ahead to ensure we don't go off course. We get clear on our intentions by looking at paths we've been on before, looking at where we'd like to land on the other side of this journey, and using that information to help us move forward. We ask ourselves, *How is this journey stretching me? What feelings come up about revisiting paths I thought I was done with, and what can I learn from this? What wisdom am I bringing with me that will light the way ahead? What do I know about myself from past journeys that assures me I have what it takes to get to the other side of this?*

I don't have to tell you how hard it is to be a single parent. Even if you co-parent, there's a transition that happens between having two adults in the home and having to rely on yourself to get it all done. I was raised by a strong single mother who was raised by a strong single mother. I knew how to single-mother well. I knew it came with sacrifices. I knew it would take the jagged edges of your life and smooth you out with each collapse that would come. I knew all of this and so I didn't panic, but my nerves were frayed. I learned that you could be exhausted and remain hopeful. Your bones can feel weak, your body can feel depleted, and you wonder if you can even take another step. Yet you know you've trained for this marathon, you know you're prepared for this path, and you know you can make it even though you'd rather not have to go through this at all. You know once you arrive on the other side, there will be nourishment and that, for a moment, you can finally take a break. You can finally slow your exasperated breaths and breathe at a normal pace. You've just left the genesis on all our paths, base camp, that presented the opportunity for you to be honest with yourself about what you need. And now that you've been honest, you can choose your intentions, and from this space, you can speak life into your world, or you can speak a demise that shrivels up your dreams before they have the chance to break ground and bloom.

You can choose to walk with the certainty that the experience you're going through will break you. It can be seductive to give up before you even start because no one wants to fail anyway. You might think that you'll never make it through and that you were wronged in being given this path in the first place. You can curse your elders for not telling it all, you can argue about how you didn't receive the education for this moment, and you can become one with the intense jealousy that courses through your veins as you watch others *appear* to glide through life like Olympic ice-skaters, as you are forced to trudge up the icy mountain with numb hands and a cold heart.

Or you can fearlessly choose hope. When people speak of living life without fear, I believe they're really asking us to choose hope. Because hope is uncertain. Hope is fallible. You can choose to walk forward, despite the circumstances weighing so heavy on your heart it feels like your chest could cave in. You can set your pride down and let people, your people, bring you offerings that will sustain you until you know what to do next. You can hold your elders with empathetic arms, understanding with grace their choices that once felt problematic, because you now know the gift and the burden of living in hope. The gift being that you believe in tomorrow being better. The burden being that you can't foresee *which* tomorrow will be better. The details of how you'll make this work are always less important than the spirit you choose to inhabit. For it is the spirit that you choose to inhabit that will help you create the details.

As I continued the five-minute walk across the parking lot, I had a moment that could only be compared to being in the desert. You're weary, and you've been walking for so long that you believe you see water, because you must believe you see water. You're running out of energy from this arduous journey and need sustenance. But you've encountered so many mirages, you don't believe what you see anymore. You don't want to be wrong. To ensure I was witnessing what I thought I saw, I reached down to the ground and picked it up, and in my hands were five crisp hundred-dollar bills.

There are miraculous moments in my life that I can't explain.

I couldn't have conjured them if I tried. Lalah Delia has a quote that says, "Your grandmother's prayers are still protecting you," and in moments like these, I lean into the knowledge that we are covered. Choose the language and connection that feels best for you, but I've realized that I never felt safer or surer of my belief that everything will work out than when I'm on a journey like this. A journey where there's no escape route, and the only way out is through. A journey where worry is more than an emotion, it's a living, breathing example of all the things five-year-old you believed were existing in the shadows beneath your bed and in the closets. It's only through turning on the lights that you gain perspective from those shadows. It's only from the other side of worry that you can allow the deep sigh of relief to move the stagnant energy living deep within your flesh. It's only then that we can know that we were covered the whole time. That we are always covered.

WALK THE TALK

Walk the Talk is where we're invited to act by using all the resources we have access to, using all the planning we did in the two previous steps, and still learning to trust that no matter the outcome, we can get through it. *Sometimes we like to act before we take the time to understand where we're starting and where we're headed. Other times we like to plan where we're headed and never take the steps. Healing is brave. Healing requires courage. And finding the strength to act is powerful. Don't take this step lightly, because if you made it here you've already done so much. Sometimes we spend years, or even decades, here. This isn't because we're slow or lazy. It's because life takes time, and we can't always control the speed. Being willing to be here for the journey, the fast ones, and the long ones, is part of our work.*

As I held the $500 in my hand, I quickly looked around me. I had an impulse to run because I felt scared. How did this money get here? I also had the intense desire to find the owner of the $500 I was gripping in my hungry hands. The bills were so clean, it was clear they had just been taken out of an ATM. Only ten seconds had passed, and I knew this money wasn't mine. And then, right out of my peripheral vision, I saw an older man picking up stuff that he'd dropped on the ground and struggling to get it all in the car. There were envelopes, and trash, and pharmacy packets. He was patting his pockets and looking around. It was his.

Have you ever had your blessing right in front of you? A job, a partner, an opportunity that YOU KNEW was going to help you. An opportunity that you'd been asking for. The very help you'd been pleading to come and relieve you of your load. But when it appeared to have arrived, you could feel, deep within a place you surely didn't want to admit, that this wasn't yours to have yet. That this moment, no matter how wonderful, wasn't your moment yet.

Before I had any time to decide what I was going to do, my legs were moving, and I was walking over to him and handing him his money. He thanked me and thanked me and thanked me. I left with my thanks and quickly turned to walk back toward my apartment before he could see the tears leave my eyes. I cried because I was sure I would be hungry that evening. I cried because I felt like an idiot for giving back what my daughter and I *needed*. I cried because I felt like a failure. I started questioning whether I'd just given away my gift. Did I make the wrong choice? I worried that I'd just given away my one chance at relief, and that I wouldn't receive another opportunity. How many times have you feared that you wouldn't receive another opportunity? How many times have you questioned whether you made the right choice? These critical moments build resilience within us. A resilience that I will honestly share I was exhausted from constantly being trained in. But the ease we desire in our lives is often created through the strength we cultivate by continuing to forge our paths despite the redirection and uncertainty.

I wish I could tell you that when I made it to my apartment, there was a check waiting for me. But that's not what happened. I followed the same routine I'd been doing for months, heading upstairs to change my clothes, heading back down to my car to pick up my daughter. But this time, before I could even close my apartment door fully to change, I dropped to my knees in despair. I was teetering on giving up my hope. I felt like an answer had been paraded in front of me as a joke that I wasn't in on. I knew that I couldn't go on like this, so when I got down to my car, instead of listening to an audiobook or the radio, I called a friend. I told her what happened, and I told her everything that had been happening. I shared that I wasn't doing as great as it may have seemed. I shared that I was eating peanut butter and four crackers for dinner. I shared about the $500 that I found and how I gave it to the person who appeared to be looking for it because it felt like the right thing to do. I shared that I wondered if it was even really his money and how I felt like a fool. I shared everything that I'd been holding in and let the waves of emotion roll out of me. And I remember her saying, "Don't worry about those five hundred dollars. I'm sorry, but don't worry. I've just sent you five hundred dollars and now you don't have to worry about it. Pay me back only when you can really do it. There's no time limit on this."

Throughout my life, I've been continuously reminded that when we're willing to be vulnerable with our people, they're able to show up and assist us on our journeys. Help isn't always going to fall right into our laps. Sometimes we have to initiate the request to receive the support. Ask yourself, are you willing to share when you are in need? Are you willing to admit that you don't know what to do? There is freedom in not knowing. Because someone else knows and can share it with you. The qualifications you think you must have and the person you think you must be? That may all be a story. I have learned that people are waiting to help us when we're willing to ask. Yes, you may still have to work. Yes, you may still have the full responsibility. But they've lessened the load. You don't always have to carry it all alone.

As I reflect on this moment now, it occurs to me that finding that $500 on the ground and experiencing that second of promise only to give the money away thirty seconds later started a revolution within me. It forced me to overthrow the system set up within me that confined me to figuring out my problems *on my own*. Like a wrecking ball, that experience broke through all those walls that I'd been hitting when trying to get to the other side on my own. Hope isn't something that we carry alone. Hope is communal. Hope is shared. That's why we feel at home with people who know the kind of suffering we've endured. That's why we cry when we see people win against the odds. On tough journeys, we ask others to tell us their stories because we want to know what hope they carried with them. We want validation that it's okay to feel like hope has forgotten you exist. We want to know what hope remained with them on the other side.

That $500 from my friend didn't solve all my problems. But it helped empower me to find new ways to fix them. It's hard to walk when we are silent about the battles we're fighting. Walking the talk isn't just about speaking up; it's also about allowing support in, in the same way you'd show up for someone you cared for. It's the quintessential thing we fear, being seen as we really are. When I am scared to be seen, I remind myself of how lonely it is to believe that I'm in this world by myself. I remind myself that my ability to thrive is dependent on knowing there will be lighthouses on my path. Lighthouses traditionally warn us about the dangers that lurk, remind us to stay aware of the direction we're headed in, and tell us when it's safe to keep going. The map of my life is filled with lighthouses that have illuminated the dark, winding roads that at some points seemed to never end. I want you to know that even if you can't see it yet, there's a lighthouse ahead, waiting to support you and gently direct you as you walk along.

LESSONS LEARNED

When we're near the end of a journey, we can either return to where we started, now equipped with new wisdom we've gained, or we can begin an entirely new journey. With new lessons learned, we reframe the idea that experiences must be a success or a failure and instead hold a new truth, that we grow either way. Here we keep our focus on what we've come to understand about what we need, how we've grown, and who we are. Our wisdom is birthed in these four places. We can be tricked into believing that it's not until we cross the finish line that lessons are learned, but from the beginning through the end we get wiser and acquire knowledge that's churned into wisdom. Wisdom is not an ending place. Our wisdom continues to grow if we are willing to admit that we don't know it all. There will be times when you're nudged by loved ones to share your wisdom, and you will know without a doubt what is needed on their paths because you've lived it. You'll know what you need if you revisit those journeys yourself as well. And then, there will be adventurous moments that mirror jumping out of a plane. You have all the safety equipment and yet you still don't know what you'll encounter because even the most well-planned experiences can be unpredictable. This is also our work. This is also the evidence of growth and wisdom.

When I chose this story to open this book, I grappled with the fact that I wouldn't be able to share a bow-wrapped, happy-ever-after ending. And that's what so many of us believe arriving on the other side of hard times is, right? We want to hear the win, we want to hear the relief, we want the ending of a '90s rom-com. We want life to change its mind about this tough lesson it handed us, jump in a taxicab and speed down the street to stop us, and serenade us and beg us for forgiveness after the hell it put us through. But it's important to know that truth, and joy, and growth can exist in the most complex parts of our lives. There can be joy on the way to light. That's the real fairy tale.

Even though I overcame a major obstacle in feeling safe enough within myself to share my struggles with my friend that day, I continued to struggle emotionally and financially for some time. The truth is, I'd arrive on the other side of one problem, only to find another one waiting for me. It felt like I was constantly going through pit stops, getting refueled and put back together for the next lap that I'd have to make. And that made me worry that there wasn't enough optimism in this book, that it was too shadowy, and that you wouldn't see the possibility for yourself. But then I remembered what I know to be true about worry. That it's often made up of stories that are filled with worst-case-scenario fears and insecurities that keep us from exploring the truth that we *can* control. Allowing the sun to shine on the deepest and darkest truths and experiences that I've pulled through is growth. It means I am soft enough to be vulnerable. It means that I am free enough to speak truth and share what it was like on the way to joy. It means I get to share the story of reclaiming myself and the triumph of still being me. That those times didn't break me.

That I still believe in hope and love and joy, even after it all. This is what your journeys offer you too.

Be proud of who you've become! Hold space for every decision you thought would break you. Hold space for every decision you had to learn and grow from. Hold space for every intentional decision that you thought was smart so of course it had to work out, but it didn't. Even the intentional decisions fail sometimes. To still be walking our paths is to know that we are still breathing, and that is the gift. To be alive and free to do it again.

On the other side of this experience, I truly just want to give younger-single-mom me a hug. She was so lonely, she was so tired, and she was so unsure of what to do. For you, when you look back at your journey, you may want to hug you too. And maybe say thank you? Thank you for not giving up. Thank you for doing the best you could. Thank you for getting up and going to that shitty job even when it was tough. Thank you for not packing your things and walking out of said shitty job, because you needed the income. Thank you for still going for your dreams even when you felt like you were in hell. Thank you for finding a therapist or coach or book, so you didn't completely fall into that hole that you were teetering on the edge of. When you look back, what are you thankful to yourself for? What did you bring yourself in moments of doubt or despair?

We only know what we've seen, what we've experienced, and where we've journeyed. When we witness our journey as the surveyor, looking at where we've been, where we are, and where we want to land, we get a new perspective that enriches our capacity for blossoming. From this point of view, we are fortunate. We reap the benefits of empathy, perspective, and the maturation that happens when we take space to observe. We learn the benefits of slowing down before responding. We learn that we're not in a race after all. We aren't plodding along. We're on the stroll of a lifetime.

Here's what I know. I know that we're stronger than we believe. I know that we're more capable than we understand. And I know that we often need a reminder of our true essence. When we map out our key moments in life, the moments that felt special and the times we learned to trust ourselves because it was all we could do, we build self-belief. This is where our freedom lives. Let's free ourselves. Together.

2

EVERY STORM
RUNS OUT OF RAIN:
ON THE JOURNEY
OF GRIEF

At least once a week, I yell out to my husband from wherever I am in the house and ask, "What did it feel like outside?" He's usually the first person to go out because he walks the dogs while I get the kids ready in the morning. He also has a unique understanding of how cold I'll be, aka how much I'll complain if I'm not dressed properly. I know there's a weather app that gives me all this information, but I want to know what it *felt* like to him. If the weather app shows sun all day but he walks outside and says it *feels* like it might rain, I know what that means, and I trust his feeling and bring my umbrella. Because this feeling he's describing is one you gain *only from experience.* This feeling is one that you earn on a day when you're unsure why the clouds are heavy, you don't understand the thick humidity weighing down the air, and you're not adept at recognizing the smell of the air before it pours. And because you're not familiar with those signs, the signs that show up before a storm, you get caught off guard and unprepared. Smack in the middle of it.

When we meet grief for the first time, it can feel just like we're caught in the middle of a storm, one that we had no idea was coming. And no idea how long it will last. The last time I saw my grandmother, I knew it was the last time. Before I saw her, I had no indication that this was the case. She wasn't sick and there weren't any fact-based indications that supported the feeling I had. I'd even made plans to see her when I'd be visiting New York again in a few weeks. But my soul knew those plans wouldn't happen. As we sat on our visit making drop biscuits and talking about music, it was easy to try to ignore this inkling. But when I mapped this experience out, searching for answers as I healed, I gained full understanding of this knowing and how it prepares us as the next storm arrives.

BASE CAMP

That entire year, I kept speaking with her like I knew time was running out. Being that this was my first experience with death, I was unaware of the energetic sensitivity my intuition could rise to. At base camp, grief feels like more than a journey; it weathers you like a battle. Think about the feeling of being powerless for a moment. No one wants this. There is a fear and rage in being without power. We want to know who took it and we want to know how we'll survive without it. Much of our wellness language, including my own, is curated around the experience of reclaiming our power. From society, from our families, and from any place we've unknowingly given it away. But grief doesn't strip us of our power. It takes away our armor. We still have fight in us, if we need it, but for the most part we feel like tired warriors walking uphill toward the next front. We drag our baggage because it's gotten too heavy to carry on our backs. In this powerless position, we're not admitting defeat, but we're accepting loss. *We can lose without having failed.* There doesn't have to be anyone to blame, and this is hard. We've been taught to figure out whose fault it is, so we can be free. But if it's no one's fault, how do we move forward? This is part of our work too.

I believe that in her very protective and loving way her soul reached out to let me know to savor our last moments together. And to try to prepare me for something I could never be prepared for. I believe we all have coding inscribed within us, that if we're open, it will allow us to communicate clearly to each other without ever having to speak out loud the words we'd never want to say anyway. I believe that's why I asked her every question I'd always wanted to know that last afternoon we sat together, and truly my only regret is that I didn't record our conversation, even though I can still hear her answers. I can also still hear her questions.

Dr. Christopher Kerr, the CEO and chief medical officer at Hospice and Palliative Care in Buffalo, New York, has done extensive research on the dreams and visions that take place for those who are dying before they pass away. His research discusses end-of-life experiences that patients encounter as they get closer to death. These experiences can take many forms, with the dying vividly recalling loved ones or even traumas.

During our last conversation, my grandmother began to ask me about my grandfather and great-grandmother, her mother, who'd died many years before. This wasn't the first time that she'd brought them up, in fact we talked about them both many times. But usually, she was sharing information with me about past experiences. Like a story she once told me about a back-to-school shopping trip for my mom with my grandfather, where his parked car started slowly drifting down a hot New York City summer street while he was in a store, and she had no idea how to stop the car. She never learned to drive, nor did she really need to in Brooklyn. It was a terrifying and exhilarating experience for her, trying to figure out how to stop this big car. My grandfather eventually came out and helped. This story used to crack us both up when she would tell it to me. But this time, the questions she asked me had a different energy. She shared that she'd been dreaming about them and that the dreams felt real. I didn't have Dr. Kerr's research at the time, but I could sense that what she and I were sharing while talking about her dreams was a sign. And for a long time, I blamed myself for not understanding those signs clearly. I originally felt that I missed the sign that could've saved her life, rather than taking the sign as the spiritual message of preparation that it was.

When we're in the thick of grief, it's helpful to have language that describes what we're going through, even if we don't learn the language until after the fact, like I did with Dr. Kerr's research. It keeps us from creating stories where we wind our words into tales that keep us stuck in beliefs or versions of the truth that aren't helpful or even accurate. And if we learn the language after we've already created stories, this knowledge helps us gently unravel the safety nets we've created in these stories and replace them with truths. When we're in grief, we seek to understand why things happened the way they did, and any knowledge that can bring calm to the frazzled parts of our being is welcomed. Is there language that you're seeking for the grief you've experienced? What story are you telling yourself that you could be free of with a deeper understanding?

INTENT

Grief, like many things on the journey, is an invitation to go inward. But not just within yourself. Because if you spend too much time alone, while grief is visiting you, you'll find yourself so lost that the only thing you can do is take a seat and ignite your flare gun so that help can come find you. Being alone is a real temptation, but the invitation is to dwell in the powerless feeling that grief brings so you are soft enough to be transformed and held. It's an invitation to plot a new path, one where, perhaps, everything you thought you knew has changed. It's a path that rocks you, and the invitation is to find a way to steady yourself again.

Personally, I didn't know what loss looked or felt like, because grief and I were just being introduced. I didn't understand what to do with all the intuitive information I could feel. I didn't understand how to cope with the deep sadness and the desire to numb in any way I could.

We don't arrive at grief bright-eyed and bushy-tailed. We

don't stand there like children on the first day of kindergarten, excitedly checking to see if we have what we believe we need to get started. We whimper over like newborn pups who were dragged here by the scruff. It's the preamble. And like any beginning there are parts we wish we could skip. At most jobs, we've encountered that annoying co-worker who always plays devil's advocate, sharing a new unhelpful comment while loudly chewing their mouthful of food, when everyone is just trying to find a solution and, ultimately, go home. Fear is the annoying co-worker. If you look at a map of your life in moments of grief, you can see the instances where fear tried to freeze you in place. The moments when fear tried to fool you into believing that because you were vulnerable, you couldn't have moments of triumph. When fear pops up with its know-it-all personality and says, "I don't know how much more you can take. This seems like too much. You're not strong enough for this. You're not equipped for this. You won't make it," it gives you pause. You think about the hill you've just climbed and all the journey you still have left. You think about how this journey of grief seems everlasting. Even though you don't trust your annoying co-worker's comments, and even though no one asked for them, fear makes a damn good point. You've just started, and you're already wiped. Fear's right, how much more can you take? The shock alone was enough.

This is a pivotal moment because we can make the mistake

of *believing* fear. When we believe fear, we don't trust ourselves, and our decisions often reflect this. Everything feels sporadic, rushed, and overwhelming. But there is another choice. The other option is to make space for our friend intuition to have a seat at the table.

Intuition is your wingman, and its job is to help you discern which direction to go in next. But when intuition feels a big shift coming, like a personal GPS, intuition warns us by giving the signal that the turn is coming up way before we reach the exit. Sometimes this early warning can feel scary. Having the sense that my grandmother was dying was not something I wanted to hear or understand, so I didn't sit with it. I pushed that feeling down and away because it felt safer to ignore. When we get an early message, and we lack the experience of being able to understand the unseen, we don't know that it's time to pay attention. So we almost miss it. Or we miss it completely. And there's grief in that too. *What would've happened had we known what was up ahead?* Learning that we can always circle back takes love and compassion. Being willing to go back and retrieve wisdom is a brave feat. But no longer carrying the stories of what you feel you ruined and instead carrying the truth with you, like a scripture there to guide you as you go? Now, this is growth.

We'll all experience the grief of losing someone we love at some point in our lives, even though most of us never want to face that truth. And we won't always have a sense that the person is going to die beforehand. I've learned to understand how much of a gift these signs are. The other truth is that we'll all encounter grief that has nothing to do with death. Grief of all sizes is waiting for us on the other side of a relationship ending, or a job loss, or a new baby, or a child growing up, or turning an age that you never got to see your parent live to. There is grief in celebration and there is grief in disappointment. I remember taking a class about drinking and driving when I was in the military. Every new airman had to take the course as a deterrent to driving under the influence. During a portion of the class, we were asked to put on different glasses, so we could see what it really looked like when you were driving at different alcohol levels. It was mind-blowing that most of the glasses, even with the smallest amounts of alcohol in the system, still affected my vision. I was not able to see as clearly as I could when those glasses were off. In grief, even with the smallest amount in your system, your vision is often disoriented. It's not that we can't see clearly, although this is sometimes true too, but we see everything with new meaning. Moments that barely had any significance, after grief, can mean more than anything in the world. What have you learned about yourself or the world through the eyes of grief?

So many of us are walking paths of grief. Grief from marriages we wanted to last forever. Grief over versions of ourselves that we'll never get to be again. Grief over getting older and grief over those we love not having the chance to grow old. We often try to tame grief, keeping it from being its wild, undomesticated self. But grief often requires being in the discomfort of massive change. Even if it's change we want, like a new relationship, baby, job, or move.

It can be powerful to ask yourself questions like:

- When I've experienced grief in the past, what felt hard? What did I learn? What was I not expecting?
- In what ways, if any, have I ignored grief?
- Are there parts of me that feel grief isn't fair? Why?
- Are there ways that grief changed my heart? How (if any)?
- Did grief introduce me to new practices, tools, or ways of connecting with myself that I'm grateful for?

Grief is a journey we'll all walk. Understanding our needs while we're on the path is healing.

WALK THE TALK

When I walked away from her that last time, I looked back to wave, as I'd done thousands of times over my life, but this time our eyes locked and her expression confirmed that she understood something more about our parting than I was able to fully accept or tune in to. I always wondered what my expression told her, despite my smiling and waving. Her expression was one I'd never seen on her face in my life; with all that we'd been through, I never saw that look. And even though my mind hadn't caught up with what my soul knew, *my body reacted*, and the moment I stepped outside, no longer in her physical presence, a cry came up out of my throat as a scream, and I wept as if she was already gone. I cried all the way home on the train. I want to emphasize again *that my body reacted to something my mind couldn't even conceptualize*. How often are you—are we—ignoring what your body is telling you? What would we gain if we listened? If we paid attention? If we worshipped our reactions with the same emphasis that we place on understanding how other people feel? As my heart started grieving what my mind could not believe, just eighteen days later, my grandmother became my ancestor.

In distressing situations, you'd like to choose your intentions before you start your journey, so you know where you want to land on the other side of it. But through the eyes of grief, I couldn't. I was pulled here by the scruff, kicking and screaming. It took me years of walking on this path, and revisiting where I walked, and understanding the paths that I crossed for me to move from self-blame to acceptance. If we traced her death through every moment in my life thereafter, there would be a road that you could take right back to the moment I found out she was gone. Everything felt connected to her loss. I was heartbroken and moving on felt like disloyalty. I remember feeling betrayed that the world seemed to continue to go on. The same TV shows playing, restaurant reservations, emails, checking in on status updates at work. Didn't everyone realize a giant had left the Earth?

Grief can feel like a freeloading companion that we can't get rid of. It's with us at work. It's with us even if we fall in love. And it takes so much of our energy. But we can decide to surrender to the process of grief without abandoning our light. Knowing this helped me release the self-pity that my grandmother truly would've rolled her eyes at. Not because she wasn't empathetic toward me, but because she would've wanted me to get on with it. I'd always ask her how she was doing and she'd often reply, "I'm still kicking, but not too high." She spent her life indirectly teaching me to focus on the fact that the leg was still working, honey! Not on the fact that a split was near impossible.

Even though the journey that I shared with my grandmother on Earth had ended, she was still with me as a guide. My new mission was staying grounded to the earth beneath me without the person who I believed was the force of gravity itself. Have you ever been anchored by someone's love? If so, you know how hard it is to take those first small steps without them. The beginning felt like I'd failed before I'd even begun. I had to lure myself back to hope. I had to choose the path toward joy, even though I'd forgotten the road existed. I had to rely on others to walk with me, their light showing the way for us both, reminding me that this path wasn't quicksand that would swallow me whole. If I let it, this life experience could lead me to a deeper connection to myself and everything in my world. I'd have to be willing, though.

When the author Elizabeth Gilbert lost her love Rayya, she shared this about grief on her Instagram account:

> *Grief says: "She's gone, and she's never coming back." I reply: "I am willing for that to be true." Grief says: "You will never hear that laugh again." I say: "I am willing." . . . This is the job of the living—to be willing to bow down before EVERYTHING that is bigger than you. And nearly everything in this world is bigger than you.*

You must ask yourself if you are willing. Willing when the times are hard. Willing when it's easier to be numb. Willing when you want to walk away. Willing when you wake up and forget what happened and you must remind yourself all over again that it's real. Willing to do it for yourself because no one else can walk this path for you; even the people who are experiencing the same loss with you will have their own journey to travel. You are plotting your own path. You get to choose when the walking begins. Take the first step tired. Take the first step with no idea whether you have the strength to lift your foot for the second step. This is your work.

To be a living example of her love was my desire. To take the baby steps that would lead to bigger steps, that would lead to a stride where without a doubt she would've yelled out "Look at the hips on you," would have to be my sermon. Regulating my nervous system would take determination. It would also mean remembering what I already knew to be true. During thunder-and-lightning storms, my grandmother would instruct me to turn off all the electricity. We'd go through the house, switching off each lamp, and as I ran over to our larger-than-life wooden TV to push in the knob, it would buzz loudly as the picture slowly faded to black, a serenading sound of silence. I never liked this hushed ritual because I was terrified of storms. I rather welcomed the distraction of TV or the radio. Have you noticed that when storms show up in your life, you welcome the distractions too?

I remember her rocking in her chair and looking like the silence gave her immense peace.

She'd looked over at me, taking a break from staring out of our tenth-floor apartment window, which in my mind meant we were only centimeters from the lightning in the sky. As she rocked in her chair and waved her fan to cool her face, she said, "God is here even when it's storming. We're safe and the storm will be over before you know it." Then she smiled at me with a knowingness that said "it's all okay" rather than "it's all *going* to be okay."

One of my favorite grounding practices to share in workshops and do myself is the self-hug. You fold your arms across your chest, and then grab each arm with a gentle squeeze. And you hug yourself. When you breathe in, you say, "I am safe." When you breathe out, you say, "It's all okay." We're not lying to ourselves. This practice invites us to speak what we desire if it doesn't feel true. I used this often during that time of grief. I was learning to anchor myself. I was learning to trust my ability to calm my system all on my own. I was learning to trust that I could get myself through unimaginable times. And the truth is that you can do this too. You can. This is the remembering. I'd already learned that I was safe in myself. I'd already learned I could find peace within me by choosing to turn off everything and getting still when it rains. I'd already learned how to reset. I already knew how to get to the light again.

In one of my favorite interviews, Dr. Maya Angelou shares, "There's a country song out now, which I wish I'd written, that says, 'Every storm runs out of rain.' . . . No matter how dull and seemingly unpromising life is right now, it's going to change. . . . But you have to keep working." We don't keep going because we must; we keep going because we want to. When we're walking up that hill, baggage in hand, tears streaming down our face, we can get confused about the mission. We think we're walking up that hill because there's no other choice. We curse the hill and march along as if we've been given orders. But it's only once we're on the journey that we begin to see all the other paths we could've taken. We talk to people who are stuck in grief that claimed their life decades prior. We speak to people who have chosen to remain in the past that they had with the person, or job, or partner, or previous life that they loved. We encounter people who've tried with all their might to look grief in the face and can't. It takes bravery to decide to start a new career when your children leave the nest and go off to college. It takes courage to go on a first date after your divorce. It takes strength to laugh during the pain. To believe that the sun will shine again is all we can do. And of course, we know that it indeed will.

LESSONS LEARNED

While writing this chapter, I observed the way I still carried language that placed blame on me for something that was not my fault. We often punish ourselves, even when we're not wrong, because we hope to beat others to the punch. If I'm already tearing myself apart, then no one else will have to do it. This cycle of self-harm often comes from being taught through penalization rather than learning lessons to have a deeper understanding. But we can liberate ourselves and restore our dignity by allowing the guilt and the fear that come with grief to be emotions we're experiencing, rather than observing these feelings as ugly definitions of who we are.

In bell hooks's renowned book *all about love*, she shares, "The practice of love offers no place of safety. We risk loss, hurt, pain." There will never be a way to control the feelings we have when grief arrives. When we show up and love others with the whole of ourselves, we are saying yes to the possibility of grief. This is the risk. This is living.

There is suffering in grief and yet grief doesn't come solely for suffering. Grief is a moment of pause, acknowledging that a cosmic shift has occurred. In the beginning, the pause is vast, stopping our whole world. But the longer we walk, the smaller the pauses, even though the emotional connection can remain just as grand.

This journey reminds me that growth can come from looking back at your past. We don't want to get stuck on those old roads, but we can revisit them for reminders when we need new direction. There are lessons in what's behind us; the past isn't there for us to only notice our perceived "mistakes." This is an important reminder for you during those moments when you're tempted to beat yourself up for what you think you should've already healed. There is beauty in returning.

Although I've climbed many hills on this grief journey, I have found that the arrival is always a new base camp for me. I begin a new phase of grief every time I land. There was the phase where I had to get used to the holidays without my grandmother and I didn't want to celebrate because nothing felt the same. There was the phase where I couldn't visit Brooklyn because it brought so much sadness. There was the phase where I learned that the holidays were a way to keep her and the traditions we had close. There was the phase where visiting Brooklyn reminded me of all the good times. Grief has many phases. There are parts of our past that we may never get over. There are times when what we've gone through feels just as fresh as it did when it first occurred. Every time I experience something exciting, I wish I could call her. I still can't visit her grave.

But we can choose to bring joy with us now. We can release our vow to grief and take an oath to willingness.

This part of my map is still unfolding. We don't have to unearth every part of our lives and break it down to the minutiae to say "we are healing." But be open to the stories and experiences that have directions to where you want to go. As I learn more, I add new roads that help me move forward. Backstreets that help me avoid congestion and have access to flow. Bridges that help me cross over experiences I'd rather not revisit. This is where I find my peace.

We can't control all that's coming our way. But we can begin to learn how to be there for ourselves when and if really hard times come. And when you don't have the answers, don't be afraid to yell out and ask for the temperature to someone who is willing to brave the weather and tell you how it feels. So, you know what you need to begin again.

3

THE DOORS:
ON SURVIVING
THE JUNGLE +
FORGIVENESS
AS A SALVE

When I was in Girl Scouts, we did a field trip to the fire department. This was one of the coolest trips I can remember. We tried on their uniforms and I remember being legit confused by how heavy they were. How were they able to run so fast with clothing that had to weigh a ton? We got to slide down the pole, which honestly felt like a huge perk of the job. I don't know if the pole was as high as it remains in my mind, or if the memory is still from my perception in my tiny younger self's body. And we even got to sit in the fire truck. I still remember how hot it felt when my legs hit up against those metal seats. The firefighters' job is to save people in the unkindest conditions. To run into a burning building goes against every instinct that I believe most of us have. Unless, of course, we believe it's our purpose to rescue people. We'll put it all on the line if, deep within our core, we believe this is who we are.

I used to believe my role was to rescue people, although not as a firefighter. The exchange of giving up my energy for the validation of the rescued person felt equal, even though it was depleting my soul. It was never directly said to me that I should save people, and yet I knew they wanted me to be strong and support them. I knew they wanted me to do life on their behalf. I knew they wanted me to carry their burdens. I thought this was my gift.

Having grown up with an alcoholic family member I'll call Steve in my home for a large part of my childhood, I believed I successfully escaped those years and everything in them when I left them behind. I created a different life for myself and yet the desire to save people and forget myself in the process came crawling through every crack and surface it could find. Sometimes we misunderstand our purpose and believe that we're not only here to walk our path, but to carry others' burdens and walk theirs too. No matter how it derails us.

As a child, I witnessed a lot of chaos that I couldn't explain. I loved Steve, who was incredibly kind when he wasn't drunk. And I believe codependency lives in-between the place where you are so fed up that you don't care that they're sleeping outside tonight, you just need a moment of peace, and the place where you can't sleep because you don't know if they'll ever make it home safe. This duality is so toxic, if an outsider walks into your home, the tension is so thick that it's like inhaling smoke. It's a tightly guarded secret and yet everyone knows something isn't right. If we should gain the strength to part our lips and speak of it, then we'd have to do something about it, so it always felt much safer to talk about nothing at all. To pretend that all was well when they finally had a few sober days or months in a row. We love them, we empathize with them, we protect them, and we pay the price when they continue to hurt us. My grandmother once said to me, "I hope he doesn't fall asleep with that cigarette in his mouth and burn the house down." This is the torture of this kind of chaos. Waiting for the embers to drop and ignite everything your lies are built on.

I wanted nothing more than to run far away from that time. I moved out of my house on my eighteenth birthday, with the hope that my life could reflect my dreams, instead of my reality being a nightmare. Even though I love my family deeply, I knew I needed to go. Have you ever made the decision to distance yourself from a situation, even though you loved the people involved? All I'd ever seen was what happened when you didn't leave. So I figured running away *had to be better.* Later in life, I read a quote from the book *The Body Keeps the Score* that stopped me right in my tracks: "One day he told me that he'd spent his adulthood trying to let go of his past, and he remarked how ironic it was that he had to get closer to it in order to let it go." My eighteen-year-old self thought the feelings of terror, trauma, and anxiety were present only if I stayed in that house. I didn't know those feelings would follow me on my path, so much a part of me that I couldn't escape them in the same way that we can't escape our shadows. It wasn't my job to escape like a fugitive under the guise of a new identity. It was my job to face things and rise, to live and to thrive.

BASE CAMP

Surviving is the act of remaining alive despite what is being thrown in your way. In survival mode, we don't approach life with deference; we ferociously meander from place to place, willing to do anything we need to hold on, because we must.

This is not abundance, although we can find glory here. The glory that we find while surviving can keep us comfortable enough. We get *some* of what we need and feel grateful. But crossing from surviving into peaceful living can feel like a stretch. What about the people who don't want to come with us? What about the people we can't save? How will we make it on our own when we've never seen it done? Can I be the first?

When we decide to leave survival mode behind and walk the path toward peace, we're learning to leave the jungle. We're reprogramming ourselves. We're giving our nervous system the message that it's safe to live out loud. We do this despite the people around us who are convinced we're making ourselves prey. "We're in the f'ing jungle," they say. "Have you lost your mind?" And know this more than you know anything: You haven't lost your mind. You've just chosen new thoughts.

Beginning again is where your power lives but it's also a seat of fear. You're choosing to bravely move on, knowing that only the unknown is ahead. You're choosing to be excited about the future, even though the past has taught you not to get your hopes up. You're choosing to shut down the notion that you're prey in a jungle. The unknown path ahead does not make you the hunted. Base camp provides the opportunity to release the conviction that you are at war with the world. That you are nothing but game to the bloodthirsty savages around you.

There's a difference between discernment and fear. The latter comes from scarcity and breeds competition, dysfunction, and comparison. It's hard to trust from that space. It's hard to let people show up for you from that space. We survive from that space, but not in the way Gloria Gaynor sang about; we just exist during hardship. What if you began again from the energy of flourishing? Yes, the path is not always easy, but the song that you hum along the way can be one that reminds you that you will make it to the other side.

I remember asking my grandmother if she had any regrets while we easefully chatted one day. "I do have lots of things I wish I would've made time to do. I've always wanted to travel. I've always wanted to learn to drive. To see more," she replied. My mind wound over the time that had been poured into ensuring that Steve never fell asleep with that cigarette in his mouth. How she'd become a firefighter just like the folks on my Girl Scouts trip. There in case of emergency. I could often see her pain of feeling like she had to be home, to ensure the world around her didn't burn down. Even though your situation may look nothing like my grandmother's, the energy of not living your life fully may feel the same. The regret may feel the same. But the good news? If you're reading this, you're not out of time. Write this down where you can see it: **There's still so much time to make my dreams come true. I just have to start. My life is waiting on me.**

My grandmother looked over at me and smiled. "You have done so much in your short life. I love that about you," she said to me. I held on to these words so tightly, and still do. No one could ever be harder on me than I am on myself, and reminding myself that the movement I'm making matters, and that it mattered to her, is one of the most special parts of my life.

You may relate to being hard on yourself and not recognizing the growth that you've made in your own life. I hope you hold on to these words. Every step you've taken matters. I also recount those words when I need to jolt myself back to the reality of what I've been doing with my time. Is too much energy going into others? Do I need to let go? Often, the answer is yes, I needed to let go, long ago. Where do you need to let go?

INTENT

Even though we know that everyone isn't coming with us on our journeys, we still hope that our new way of being will serve as an incentive for them to try to walk with us. As someone who was untangling the "system of savior" that was encoded within me, this was the hardest part. Learning to fully release the desire to try to make others live the life that we've chosen for ourselves and instead encouraging and supporting them to make the changes that would be sustainable and best for them is healing. It also gives us freedom to get clear on what we want.

If our focus is solely on others, then we lack space for ourselves. Like sponges, if we soak up everything around us, we'll have no room for anything when what we want comes along. And what do you want? Where do you want to end up? What are the juicy parts of life that you're not even ready to admit, because you're still working up the courage to say it out loud? How do you want to move through the world? What do you want your life to feel like? What do you want to be excited about the moment your feet hit the ground in the morning? Our intentions live here in the answers to these questions. We have to be willing to make the tough choices and walk the paths that get us where we want to be.

When we start to feel the exhilaration of our future approaching, those old beliefs that we had with the people or experiences we left behind may come and visit. Their ghosts fill our space with memories of who we were when we were with them, and we get lost. We forget our becoming. We forget our lessons. We forget the hills we've climbed and the mountains we've surpassed. If our intention is to have a full life of friends and wonderful events to enjoy, we can't listen to the ghosts that come forward and say, "But remember when it felt like no one liked you?" Survivor's guilt can do that. It can make you think that you "got away" by chance and cause you to question your worthiness. Survivor's guilt will try to convince you that you should've never made the choice to resist conformity. That you're lost and need to go back to what "you know." That you should go back to "who you really are." *But you are not what you've been through.* You didn't *get away*, you're returning to the true seat of who you are. You made an intentional decision to walk forward, a decision that you're continuously making with each step you take. Who you were before you knew your capacity to thrive can *never* get in the way of who you're becoming now that you know what you're really made of. It's in these moments we reach for our maps. It's in these moments our journeys can remind us of who we are.

WALK THE TALK

Even though Steve would have moments of sobriety, his drinking stands out the most as the constant state of chaos in my childhood. Throughout my adult life, I noticed how my experience with him impacted my life and relationships, and I didn't want to continue to have that be a barrier to the joy I wanted and truly felt I deserved. So, I got curious about what a journey of forgiveness could look like without ever receiving accountability, responsibility, or an apology from the person I felt was at fault.

I know alcoholism is a disease and I have so much empathy and understanding for the things that were most likely out of his control in many ways. Yet I also held (and still hold) my reality of his choices, and how I developed deep fears because of those experiences. I held so much anger about how those fears would sprout up during the most vulnerable moments and hold me hostage from allowing people to show up for me. These fears would sprout up inside me right when I needed support, love, or connection, and they kept me from allowing people to show up for me. These fears felt rooted down and they'd grow at the most inopportune times, keeping me from experiencing the softness I longed for. In those fear-induced moments, I would stand in my own way. I felt like so much of who I could've been was taken away without me ever having a choice.

I think about all I've been through in my life that was sparked by experiences I had with him. The programming that was deep within me to not trust. I've had to weigh the parts of me blaming him for what I believe he took and the parts of me that can take responsibility and change my life now. I felt like I was burdened with responsibility for something that wasn't my fault. Why was this mine to fix? It was hard not to feel like a victim. Yet a victim wasn't what I wanted to be. It made me feel exposed, and I already felt the wind enough on this path. But as I walked toward forgiveness, my own forgiveness and releasing the anger I held toward him, it was clear that, yes, his choices changed so much of my life and also, *now my life belonged to me.* When was I going to own that I belonged to a world that was fully available to me, and that nothing could be removed that was meant for me? That he couldn't derail me if he tried?

It was tough to imagine at first, because I was still depleted from the way he seemed to command the dust beneath our feet to twist and swirl around us, debris flying everywhere, leaving our eyes impaired by what we were witnessing. When the dust would finally settle, we couldn't remember which direction we were going in the first place. In one day, he could derail an entire year. The many frantic 911 calls and hospital trips. The many times I remember walking home and seeing an ambulance outside of my building, hoping it wasn't for him, but it was. The tears. The smell of urine-soaked sheets, and it felt like it took days for that stench to air out. The sound of his body hitting the hard, cold floor and the screams of everyone running to his aid. The sound of his pain as everyone tried to help while calling the ambulance. Everyone except me, because even as an adult, I would run and hide, covering my ears and crying. I was always too afraid of the sound, of the reality. The constant fear that his moments of sobriety wouldn't last long enough for things to feel normal. The shame of not being the rescuer I thought I was. The shame of never being able to have anyone over to my house because who knew what would be happening that day. The sadness in my grandmother's eyes when he decided to go back out after she begged him to stay because he'd had enough for the day. The stability he ruptured. The little me hiding behind her bed when he stumbles in, because I don't yet know what any of this means but I know I'm scared. Scared of the man that was truly kind when he was sober.

With each step that I took on this journey, I kept asking myself, Is he not to blame? If I forgive him, does that erase blame? Blame. Without it, I felt he was being let off the hook. Blame felt like the only power I had left. Have you ever been in a situation where all you could muster were the words "they did this to me"? It felt like bravery to whisper those words; it felt like karma to scream those words. I may not own the past, but with blame, I felt like the victor in the end. Was this not about who won? And what was winning?

As I'd left home at eighteen and joined the military at nineteen, far away from New York and the people who'd experienced this with me, I found myself walking this path of forgiveness and finding acceptance on my own. Clarissa Pinkola Estés, author of *Women Who Run with the Wolves*, shared: "The doors to the world of the wild Self are few but precious. If you have a deep scar, that is a door, if you have an old, old story, that is a door. . . . If you yearn for a deeper life, a full life, a sane life, that is a door."

I'd found a door. Now my work was to bravely walk through it and start my path.

You have a door. Your work is to bravely walk through it and start your path.

If I wanted to release myself from being a casualty of Steve's choices, I'd have to look at my life through a new lens. For a long time, I thought my past traumas were something that *had to happen* to me to equip me with the experiences I needed to survive. And I was tough because of it. And street-smart. The programming worked. And yet love felt foreign. I had love in my life growing up, lots of it. But it wasn't my first language. I wasn't fluent.

If we look at my map during this part of my journey, we take a deep look at the scars impeding my walk. Some wounds were so tender that I was afraid to touch them. I knew I'd wince. Understanding *why* I wanted to reframe this part of my life was incredibly important for me. I didn't want to lose myself in healing for healing's sake; that can be such a waste of our time. Most of us want to find a way to keep the past from having so much control over where we're going. We want to be able to create our future without what we've made it through hindering us. Why are you walking this path? What are you hoping to find resolution in?

We want to feel strong, but not because we're carrying heavy weight. Because we had the strength to walk a journey of healing that we knew might have moments of discomfort, and yet we endured it because of what awaited us.

We want to feel optimistic. We carried the story that where we're from was limiting where we could go. And that dampened our hope. We're ready to believe that we can create the life we desire.

We want to feel ready to not only sit at the table of abundance but to feast from it. Our gifts haven't been created to simply offer. We're allowed to enjoy them too.

We want to feel the glory of the people who came before, paving the way, rooting for us. We want to create a new lane for the people coming after us too.

Take some time to think about how you want to feel. Where do you gather your motivation? What generational blessings are you creating for yourself and perhaps people you love? What are you hoping to experience in your future because of the work you're committing to today?

LESSONS LEARNED

On the journey of finding some form of peace with Steve, I wanted to land without so much hatred and anger in my heart. This wouldn't necessarily change anything for Steve or his life, but I was sure that it would change so much for me. I didn't want little me to believe that the fear we felt could only be replaced by rage. I didn't want to be overburdened with those heavy emotions that I was carrying for both the little and the big me anymore. I wanted to give myself the peace that I so often prayed for as a child. This was the coordinate that I was changing in my soul's compass. This was how I could begin to change my life.

It's important to mention that when I talk about forgiveness with clients as a spiritual guide and coach, or even online when I release a podcast episode or post, I get tons of messages about how much pressure it creates. Forgiveness can often feel like the blame is being shifted from the person who wronged us onto us. Why do I have to work to forgive them when they wronged me? And the answer is you don't. Forgiveness is a personal choice, one that we usually make to free ourselves. We also get to choose whether we want to use the word *forgiveness*. You can choose other language that feels better for you. This is your journey. You don't have to walk through forgiveness if it feels like a step too much for you. Only choose what you need. You're still doing this walk with honor and grace every single time you show up.

For me, my first step in forgiveness was empathy. Empathy for me and for him. This turned out to be easier than I imagined, because I never felt empathy in the past. But when I removed my experience, and all the people in my family's experiences, from my mind, and I just focused on him, his life looked different to me. I didn't see him holding the reins and having full control of the mayhem. I saw the opportunities he missed out on, the pain that he might feel from seemingly not being able to control his choices, the disappointment or perhaps shame that he might struggle with. I saw the dreams that he had that could never come true. I saw the way he must've watched his life pass him by. I also thought about his generosity and the kindness that he would offer during his sobriety. None of this was an excuse for his behavior, but I saw the human parts of him too. And it helped me release anger that was holding me back from the peace I so dearly wanted in my life. *You're allowed to release the things that you feel are holding you back in your life too. You're allowed to choose empathy and accountability. We are jugglers, shifting the emotion we're holding depending on the circumstances. You can also feel empathy, accountability, and choose not to forgive or continue a relationship. You're allowed to choose.*

My next step was to get honest with myself about what forgiveness looked like. I knew that it looked like acceptance. Learning not to replay the old experiences with that glimmer of "Can you even believe that happened?" I'd often reply to myself when this occurred, saying, "Yes, Yasmine, I can believe it happened, because it did. I went through this. But I'm safe now." This acknowledgment didn't change the past, but it did release the spinning sensation of those stories replaying while simultaneously helping me gain my power back. *It's safe to accept that you went through things that were hard. You don't have to pretend hard times didn't happen. You also don't have to live in them. You're allowed to have happiness, success, and all the things that maybe at one point you didn't think would be possible. It's all available to you. And more.*

In Mark Nepo's *The Book of Awakening*, he has a passage that states, "As with so many other crucial negotiations of life, what's required is to honor what lives within us. We must bear witness to ourselves, for there is no power as embracing or forgiving as the authority of that portion of God that lives in each of us."

To forgive myself was to stand in my power. To forgive Steve was the bravest work I'd ever do. My forgiveness was evidenced by the beauty that showed up in my life, beauty that was blocked by my anger and shame. I forgave him by letting my loved ones get close, remembering that to have them and lose them would be more of a blessing than to have them and never truly experience them because of fear. I forgave him by opening my heart and loving people even when they let me down, as all humans do sometimes, even when they love us. The love in my life and relationships was blocked because I saw how someone you love could be a nightmare. But by holding on to that belief and fear, I was living the greatest nightmare, a life not filled to the brim with love. This didn't mean that his and my relationship was ever going to change. But energetically, I released the vow that I'd made to hold on to the fury no matter what. I was not here to punish him. And I wasn't punishing him; that anger was only harming me. I was free to let go. You are free to let go too.

I remember the moment when it hit me that what I'd been through was no longer holding me back the way it used to. I was spending time with my kids, and we were playing. I *love* my kids. I adore them. I am silly with them. And yet before this journey, I could feel that there were still parts of me blocked off to them. Not because I didn't want them close, quite the opposite. I didn't feel worthy of them. Unconsciously, I believed I was shielding them from the parts of me that I never wanted them to know. But as we know, when we block one part of our heart, it's hard not to block it all. And I prayed and worked vigorously to remove that barrier.

We were all just laughing and playing together and then I realized I was really letting their laughs in. Their laughs didn't have to go through the fog to get to my heart. I wasn't repelling their laughs for fear that I didn't have the capacity to hold space for their pure joy, joy that I didn't know when I was a kid. I just laughed with them. And looked in their eyes. And hugged them. And felt their love and knew that I was worthy of their love as their mom. And I'd never felt that before this journey. I knew this was the other side for me.

It wasn't until this occurred that I was finally able to begin the path of self-forgiveness. As hard as that is to admit, it's the truth, because I didn't like myself for the way that so much of my internal hurt got in the way of my mothering. I wanted to be able to fully separate my experience as a mom from my experience as an individual, and I learned that for me, it wasn't that simple. I held more empathy and compassion for me, and bucketloads more for the caregivers in my life. It helped me heal so much, seeing how tough it can be to parent. We don't have to have empathy for others to be able to hold it for ourselves, but for many of us this is the path. Don't be ashamed if the healing happens outside of you before it comes in.

Once I could feel the softening within myself, I knew I didn't need to unearth every memory that had occurred, that I had arrived at a landing place for the moment. I didn't need an apology or a deeper conversation. I didn't need anyone who was there with me to validate my experience or give me a different perspective. I wanted the wisdom and compassion to share my story without needing to tear anyone to shreds. And not because people should be allowed to get away with their wrongdoing, but because I'd worked through those tough parts for *me*.

The little me, who had stood up so bravely throughout the years, could now walk gently beside me, hand in mine, knowing that she was protected. If she needed rest, I could scoop her up gently, carrying her until she was ready to walk again. She no longer needed to be the strong one for me. She'd been walking around in heavy gear, just like firefighters do. But this was not her job. I was the one in charge of us. Tending to our needs with care, allowing tears to fall when they needed to. Allowing space to work through any concerns that come. Giving myself permission to be seen by the people who love me. Caring for myself through connection.

There is freedom in knowing that it's safe to be soft. Little you, who felt so out of control, may've thought that the only way you could ever be vulnerable was to be big, to be louder, to be the winner. To rescue and make everyone proud. Little you may have dreamed of being bigger and saving everyone. Those big dreams that our tiniest selves held don't just fall away. They show up when we grow up. And it's up to us to put them to rest. To reacquaint ourselves with what home feels like now.

I didn't realize that the accountability I needed wasn't from Steve, it was from me. This was my door to freedom. I was a savior after all. I saved myself.

Part 2

WHERE

YOU

ARE

4

BECOMING:
ON TRANSFORMATIVE
INTENTIONS

When I was first learning to meditate, it was a struggle. Before every class the teacher would ask us to find a seat and get comfortable. Reluctantly, I'd find a space, getting settled as if I'd been forced to be there. You would never know that I went on the website, found the schedule, and booked the session myself. You would never know that I was trying this new-to-me practice as a form of surrender. I was hoping to connect to the wisdom within me and learn to soften. And yet I sat in that class, week after week, very disgruntled. I didn't like meditation because it required stillness, and that felt uncomfortable to me. I didn't believe any of these modalities *worked* for "someone like me." And "someone like me" was a young woman who was not yet able to sit with herself. It was too scary to have the space to look at my life, through all the phases, and acknowledge what was in front of me. It was too scary to have the space to see storms arriving and be ready to face them. I struggled to believe that strength could come from stillness. I thought strength could only come from never stopping. Never slowing down. I'd never known a day of stillness in my life, nor in my mind, and was certain that I was strong because of it. But I came to class anyway. Something pulled me into that class every week, no matter how much I fought myself. Somehow my soul knew something that my mind didn't understand yet. Our souls always do. Like a compass, our souls always show us which way to go.

After we got comfortable in our seats and took a few cleansing breaths, my favorite part because I would always unconsciously hold my breath, we'd go through the part I struggled with the most. Setting our intentions. Every single time, I'd internally complain about what I thought was this "ridiculous" inner searching that "never led me anywhere." "Why does what I want matter? It won't happen anyway," I'd say to myself inside. I didn't understand the definition of *intention* and so I'd ask each time what *exactly* they meant by "setting intentions." They'd answer me each time, and still, I felt like it wasn't connecting. My disconnect with intentions was fear around sharing clear outcomes because what if it never happened? Now all would know. So, unconsciously, I felt it was best not to speak about it. I'd get so in my head about not being able to do this part of the practice that I'd spend the class upset. "Why can't I dream?" I'd think to myself. "Why do I keep coming to this practice that I can't stand," I'd mumble every time, class after class. And then I'd sit through the rest of the meditation practice like I'd been called to attend jury duty. So you can understand how I never would've guessed that I would write a book where one of the guideposts would be "intentions." Life is so funny that way.

Have you ever beaten yourself up when you were trying something new, because it wasn't turning out the way you envisioned it? Maybe it wasn't about intentions like mine was, but each time you tried, you walked away defeated and thought, "maybe this isn't for me," when at the same time you could *feel* this thing you were trying was very much for you. It's tough to keep going. People try to affirm us by cheering, "keep going" and "you've got this," but when you're sitting there feeling like you don't in fact "have this," it all feels forced. Fake. Wellness mumbo jumbo that makes us feel alone in the struggle with our very real feelings of failure or defeat or struggle.

But in those moments where it continues to be hard, and you keep coming back because you can feel, despite the toughness, that this journey is part of your becoming, this motivating force is an unexplainable magic that gets you to the other side. You can feel that this path of learning and trying and learning and walking, no matter how hard, is a journey that's giving you access to a heart that's open and courageous and willing to overcome the messy and beautiful path of becoming. That with each step you take, you're moving deeper into you.

That's often what we're looking for when we try something new. We're scratching the itch of our souls that is nudging us toward unapologetic living. Where we know we won't always get everything right the first time, and we're okay with it. Where we may be afraid to put ourselves out there, but we won't let that fear stop us. This nudge reminds us that we are worthy of embracing our aspirations. It's only from this loving space that those affirmations of "keep going" and "you've got this" can live and be believed.

The word *intention* comes from the Latin word *intentio*, which means "stretching or pulling." This is often what setting an intention can feel like. What we *intend* is often such a far reach from where we stand, and we're asking to be *stretched* far beyond what we can see or feel. Through intentions, we can commit to changing our beliefs and create the magic that lives inside us, making it reality. Through our intentions, we become.

BASE CAMP

As you review the twists and turns on your map, you might notice a theme in relation to your intentions. Oprah says, "I believe luck is preparation meeting opportunity. If you hadn't been prepared when the opportunity came along, you wouldn't have been lucky." To be prepared for something to occur, the intention has to be living somewhere inside us. What are the moments that you wrote off as luck that happened because you were prepared for them to happen? When were the moments that you said yes to the scary thing, to the hard thing, to the thing you wanted to quit but didn't, because you wanted the growth more?

In the book *The Body Keeps the Score* by Bessel van der Kolk, we learn about how the body and mind are connected. He shares that when we develop awareness of what we're experiencing in our bodies and understand how we're interacting with the world, we move toward freeing ourselves from the past. So, when we're dreaming up our intentions, our brains are working to visualize the desires we want, while remembering all the mucky, hard, and burdensome roads we've walked. But remember, walking is a choice. We can stop on

73

our paths and choose not to move from the situations that are plaguing us. Or we can move despite them. Even if the walk doesn't reflect your dreams yet, the walk is preparation for when the opportunity comes. And base camp is where we prepare. It's our launchpad.

Remember all the preparation that you've already done when you write off your determination as "luck." We need to remember these moments at base camp when we're contemplating a new road to travel. You need to remember that you fought, you believed, you cried, and you didn't give up. You need to remember that you'll be triumphant again.

I believe this is what kept me coming back to meditation class. As much as I complained about how I wasn't experiencing the magical things that everyone else talked about feeling when they meditated, I refused to give up. Sometimes we complain along the way, dragging our energy of defeat with us as we walk. I kept the same routine for almost a year. Coming to class, finding a seat, feeling confused about my intentions and upset about not being able to connect to myself, and leaving, dragging my defeat with me out the door.

And then in one class there was a shift. I found my seat like I always did. I felt confused and nervous about the intentions question that I knew was coming, like I always did. But this time, I knew I wanted to connect to myself. *I didn't know at the time that **this was my intention**.*

74

And during this class, instead of staying with the feeling of anger like I always did, it gave way to sadness. And that sadness gave way to tears. And when I came back to the room, opening my eyes, I realized I'd been connecting to myself all along. How wonderful it is to know that while I was dismissing the possibility of interconnectedness, I found that I was always in tune. If you feel anger, it's because you're angry. If you feel sad, it's because you're sad. If you feel distant, there may be some disconnection. None of these emotions are wrong, indefinite, or defining of who we are. They just are what they are. How freeing it is to know that even if you're at the beginning, standing at the threshold of the unknown, there is still so much possibility. Defeat isn't as permanent as it seems.

INTENT

It takes time to release the heaviness of expectation. The story of what's holding you back can feel so tightly wound around your reality, it cuts you off from witnessing anything other than what you believe to be true. I'm an overpacker when I travel. I don't enjoy realizing that I need something that I didn't bring with me. So I always bring a few extra sets of clothing. I pack "just in case" medicines and anything else that I wouldn't want to be without. Every time something is added to my "overpacking list of things I must bring," it's because of an experience I had while traveling. One time while recording video meditations for work (yes, I'm a meditation teacher now; I told y'all life can be funny), I ate something at lunch that caused an allergic reaction. As I sat recording the meditation, I could feel heat on my face and the inside of my ear tingling. It's a bit distracting to stay calm and focused when you feel this happening, so I paused and shared what was going on with everyone on set. When looking through my bag, I realized I didn't have any allergy medicine on me, so the crew ran out to get meds for me to take. It was scarier to not have the medicine when I needed it than the actual mild allergic reaction itself. Now I have allergy medicine on me wherever I go. There is always a story attached to why we do what we do. We're often trying to protect ourselves in ways we couldn't before.

This is also why, when we're on our paths, we overpack and bring stories with us that we hope will keep us informed and safe. We lug them along just in case something familiar shows up so we can immediately react. But often, these stories aren't helping us, they're weighing us down. They're making the journey longer than it must be because we're more focused on the unnecessary weight that we're carrying than on the walk itself. I truly believed meditation wasn't for me. I kept going, hoping I was wrong, that by some stretch of the imagination, something would shift. Before that last transformative class, I felt I was experiencing a *realistic limitation* that was in the way of everything that I desired from the practice. A limitation that was part of who I was and would never leave. But I was wrong, and if you believe this, you're wrong too. We are limitless. And with that knowing, we can remove anything that's in our way.

Our intention pulls us in the direction of our desires. Like a magnetic force, it reroutes us whenever we get off track. Walking with your intention doesn't mean the path will be without error or lessons, but it means that you're right where you want to be. It's the essence of leading from your heart. And I know how cliché or even corny that can sound. I know it doesn't feel natural to everyone to say something like this. When I was struggling with meditation, and I believed that "it wasn't for me," I wasn't saying this from a place of acceptance. It felt like defeat. The story that I was too hardened, or too detached, or too broken, or "too" anything to connect to myself was a false truth. I beat myself up tirelessly about not doing meditation right, because I wasn't honoring my experience. I was comparing it to what I thought *should* happen.

But you know this story wasn't about meditation at all. James Baldwin famously said, "Not everything that is faced can be changed, but nothing can be changed until it is faced." The stuckness of my thought "meditation isn't for me" was stemming from my struggle with intentions. My struggle with intentions was stemming from my fear and inexperience with saying what I wanted out loud. My fear of saying what I wanted out loud was stemming from lack of belief in my worthiness to obtain it and the real-life disappointment I'd already experienced. I kept going back to that class; I kept trying. But until I was willing to admit what I wanted, and that I would commit no matter what, I couldn't connect, because I didn't believe it was possible.

Showing up is the work, yes. But being open is critical. And don't you worry, I'm not about to hit you over the head with law-of-attraction advice. I'm asking you to look at the power that you hold. How can we become who we want to be if we don't believe it's possible before we even get started?

I finally believed in the power within me during that meditation. The same power that's within you. With tears running down my face, I looked around the room. I felt lighter. It was like I closed my eyes with the weight and opened my eyes unloaded. Connecting to myself wasn't about finding a cool string of words to put together and chant. My intention didn't need to make sense to anyone but me. Connecting to myself was as individual as my breath pattern. As my fingerprints. I was developing the power to trust that when you go inward, you'll be okay. That the softness won't break you; it will give you a place to recharge. And a place to hear, without interruption, what you have to say. In that transformative class, I released my defeat and chose my power.

If I asked you what your intention was for today, would you be able to think of the spirit you want to carry you? What do you want each day to feel like? How do you want life to stretch you? Ask. Don't be afraid to ask. Don't be afraid to say the good things out loud. Don't be afraid to request that things change immediately from the direction they're going in. Don't be afraid to want something that no one you know has ever tried to get. Too often, we're afraid of the good. Don't be afraid of the good.

WALK THE TALK

I listened to a Potter's House sermon called "Timing Is Everything," and I reflected on the importance of understanding that not only are we not exempt from good things happening at the same time as bad things, but they both take time to mature, and sometimes they show up in our lives together. The bad being ready right alongside the good. Even if you're not a person of faith, or this particular faith, this story speaks to the part of us that is worried that the bad always waits for the good to arrive and then blows everything up in our faces.

During this sermon, a parable is shared in which Jesus talks about a farmer who planted wheat for harvest, but while the farmer was sleeping an enemy came and planted weeds along with the good seeds. Once the wheat began to sprout, the weeds began to sprout as well. The farmer was asked by those working with him where the weeds came from if he was sure he sowed *good seeds*. The farmer replied that an enemy had planted the weeds among the good seeds. When they asked the farmer if they should pull up the weeds, the farmer replied, "No . . .*because while you are pulling the weeds, you may uproot the wheat with them*. Let both grow together until the harvest" (Matthew 13:25–30, NIV, italics added).

It's not abnormal to notice the weeds growing in your garden. Don't be afraid of the stumbles along your path. Set-backs aren't the end. I sat in that meditation class, mumbling my grievances, and didn't realize that my relentless bravery to keep going was planting seeds of growth right alongside the weeds that felt bigger. The seeds that you're planting can blossom right alongside the heartache, and confusion, and dif-ficulty. We're sometimes looking for ease when the stumbles remind us of the strength we have to get back up again. So we can reference our maps for guidance on how to be confidently patient while wait for blooming season.

As you walk on your journey, you'll recognize these planted stories that grow wild like weeds, taking over the entire path.

You'll take steps through them and around them, but they feel unavoidable. These stories were planted within us, but we don't have to mend them and create an environment that makes it safe for these stories to thrive. Using your energy to try to figure out how the weeds got there, why the person who planted them did what they did, and how you got them in the first place can be helpful in releasing. In some cases, we may find that we're the ones who planted the weeds ourselves, unconscious collaborators in stalling our growth. But this is not your only work.

Your work is to continue to walk, speaking your intentions out loud and preparing for abundance right alongside the weeds. This is brave and this is scary and yet this is the work. From this place you can see what's yours to hold on to and what needs to be released. Beginning your walk is the bravest step that you will take. When we look at the maps of our lives, and we reflect on these steps that we took, we'll stare in awe of our ability to be transformed through surrender. It's not our job to use all our energy to clean out the weeds. Yes, the garden will look beautiful. But we don't want to disturb our fertile ground just yet. The pain that became present once I was able to speak my intention in meditation class gave way to learning lessons that I may not have seen or understood without that discomfort. We don't need to struggle to grow, but there is often growth in the struggle. We can hold on to the wisdom we receive from hard times and release everything else. This is healing too.

As you move along your journey, the memory of these weeds may tumble across your path, whispering the haunting words of the past, and trying to get you to go back on your word to release them. These ghosts are not yours. Their home is not with you. Their stories don't belong to you. As we heal, we uproot our belief systems, disentangling them as we're left to discern what we want to hold on to. What do you want to flourish in your garden? What do you want to bloom?

If you find yourself in a space of transformation on your path, you know how cathartic it is to have what *you thought* were your beliefs plucked right from their homes to make room for new, abundant beliefs to grow. Perhaps you genuinely believed that you were too old to live your dreams, were too uneducated to start a new career, had too many partners in the past to find love now, or any other array of beliefs that limit us. A simple question, like what is your intention, can trigger our awareness to the existence of these limitations. When you plan a garden, you don't put seeds just anywhere. You plant with intention. You decide what time is best. You find shade for the seed that will need that protection. You find sun for the seeds that thrive in light. Our aspirations are no different.

LESSONS LEARNED

The first time I came back to meditation class after the transformative practice, I had nerves about something new. Was that just a one-off experience? Would I be able to find that peace within myself again? Hello, my name is Yasmine and I'm a recovering overthinker ☺.

Our job isn't to eliminate nerves, becoming robotic versions of ourselves that don't feel. Our job is to lean on tools that can support us through these emotions so we can feel safe enough to take the risk! I used a tool that was new to me, patience, and set the intention that I would be a kind companion to myself on this voyage. This intention would set the tone for any future walks. I was learning the gift of being on my side. My job was to nurture myself and show up willing to support whatever came up during the experience. This is your job too.

What I know to be true is that we're allowed to examine what we want and who we want to be, and this isn't evidence that we're wrong about our light. If we're not careful, we can look at an opportunity to grow, like the one I had while trying meditation, as an opportunity to prove that something is *wrong* with us because it's a challenge. We may see our struggles as proof of fault. "Their garden doesn't have weeds and mine does! This must mean something is wrong with my garden!" Since weeds are seen as unpleasant, we don't want them around. But weeds can often be mistaken for beautiful flowers. The garden you're comparing yourself to, as beautiful as it seems, might be full of weeds, and you wouldn't know, because *you've* deemed it beautiful. Likewise, transformative lessons won't always look the way you expect them to at first glance. Stay open.

And you're not wrong about you just because your dreams aren't here yet. You're not wrong about you just because you're realizing you need something different from your relationships or because you're learning to speak out loud. You're not wrong about you because you're still building confidence. You can meet your blessings by taking every step you can toward them. The magic is still happening behind the universal scenes. It's still happening for all of us. I believe this with all of me.

Give yourself permission to feel excited about what you want. When we feel limitless, we take the risks. We start the new project, or go on the date, or try the new business. We commit to our healing in a different way because we believe what we desire for our lives is possible, even if no one else does. Fixed limits strip us of possibility and hope. Limitless living gives us freedom.

It was this very limitless feeling that supported me through my next year of meditation, trying all different kinds of practices and finding the ones that suited me and releasing the ones that didn't without judgment. It was this very limitless feeling that guided me toward becoming a meditation teacher, immersing myself in years of teaching with spiritual teachers and guides and developing my own practice, which focuses on people who are where I was—feeling certain that meditation is not for them. I've heard hundreds of people share that they've never been able to meditate until they came to my practice. This isn't because I'm special, although I do believe we all have wonderful gifts. This is because I walked where they walked. My gift is unique because of where I've been. Do you see the beauty in this? When we survive what we were sure would break us, we build endurance for the road ahead. When we survive what we thought we couldn't, we light the way for those coming after us.

My intention in trying meditation wasn't to become a teacher, it was to connect to myself. Through connecting with myself, I found my truth, I found safety, and I found many gifts I never thought would be there. When you connect to yourself, what do you hear? What gifts break through the soil, waiting for you to nourish them into reality? What gifts or dreams are waiting for you to have the courage to speak? What intention is right on the tip of your tongue?

In the book *all about love* by bell hooks, she states, "As we move toward our desired destination we chart the journey, creating a map. We need a map to guide us on our journey to love—starting with the place where we know what we mean when we speak of love." Our maps lead us to the people, places, and experiences that foster a feeling of love in our lives. And knowing where we *intend* to go gives us a clear sense of direction and purpose. There are so many oppressive societal and economic systems that can truly be limiting, and I'm not saying we ignore that they exist. I understand their limits and constructs. But through connection to ourselves, through intentionally walking along our path, through love and acceptance of who we are, we make it to the other side.

There are times when we can't move forward because systems are holding us back. And then there are times when we can't move forward because *we* are holding ourselves back. This is a reminder to be on your side. To not be an unconscious collaborator on the journey of limitation. To choose to remove those beliefs that say you're useless. To know, as Marie Forleo says, "Your dream exists because you have what it takes to make it happen." You have what it takes. Find a comfortable seat. Set the intention, even when it's hard. Find your unhelpful beliefs and release them. And then open your eyes, ready to see the world and all it has to offer with new vision.

Meditation creates space for presence and peace, both of which support us as we journey through highs and lows. Two meditations are included in this book to help support you on your journey. You can find both in the epilogue.

86

5

ROOT PEOPLE: ON BUILDING COMMUNITY AS A CORNERSTONE

Right before I went onstage for a performance in elementary school, a "friend" looked me in the eye, in front of everyone, and said, "I knew you'd wear the wrong thing. Your shorts are so stupid. Are you really that poor?" We'd decided on black shorts for our performance, and I'd cut those shorts from a pair of old jeans that were unwearable because they were high-waters, and the cuts were un-even. We didn't have a washer and dryer in my house, which was not uncommon in New York, so washing them for the frayed look and having them dry in time was out of the question as well. It didn't occur to me to fold up the shorts so they'd look better; I was only twelve, so not totally fashion savvy yet. Said "friend" did help me roll up my shorts, and we went onstage.

Despite this interaction, I still pined for her acceptance. I thought winning her over meant belonging. I wanted to be well liked by people even when I wasn't well treated. So many of us ignore the obvious signs that a relationship is not healthy because we are convinced that we can convert the person to think differently about us. Often, we do this because we've been in situations growing up where caretak-ers were people we'd have to perform for to receive love. My tendency to work hard to befriend people whom I should walk away from kept me from the connection I wanted. I focused my energy on charming people who barely liked me instead of connecting with the people who did. And I know I'm not alone in this. There may be relationships that you're in right now where you're teetering on liberating yourself from people that no longer feel like allies. Releasing those draining relationships is the key to letting go of a lot of drama that's being caused not by their behavior, but by your participation in staying despite their behavior. This letting go is also the key to experiencing the beauty of connection and support in friendships, a part of healing that has supported me dearly.

I've always made friends easily and been able to maintain long-term friendships. But during my twenties, I could see that what I wanted in friends was changing. For one, I'd started my healing journey, and what I once believed filled me up, like being at a club the night before and not remembering a thing that happened because of how much partying I did, was no longer doing it for me. I wanted more out of my connections. But I didn't understand the ways my needs were changing in my relationships, and I was also stuck in many stories. One story was that friendship had changed only because of the area I was living in. I was far from my closest friends in New York, and the culture was different in DC than it was in my home of origin. I believed the bumps in the road I was experiencing weren't about the relationships themselves, but instead were just a matter of my location. "When I move back to New York things will be so much easier," I'd say to myself and others, watching my life pass me by as I waited to move back "home." Have you ever waited for things to change, forgetting that it's you who's in charge of sparking the change you want?

BASE CAMP

I'm not the only one intrigued by these words by Mary Oliver: "What is it you plan to do with your one wild and precious life?" This inquiry asks us to look in the mirror. And most of us don't want to see our reflections. I know I wasn't ready to witness my truth in my twenties. Hell, it's hard to look in my thirties sometimes too. The mirror is an exact likeness of what appears. We can't deny what we see, so we prefer to avoid the looking glass.

I felt like I wasn't living; I was waiting for life to begin. In some magical way, I anticipated that Oz would turn the switch, and everything—my life, my connections, the fun, the joy—would just start *happening*, without my participation. But life doesn't work that way. Relationships don't work that way. They take effort. If I wanted to beam when I talked about the work I was creating in the world, and have friends who were excited about my path, not people who appeared to have an existential crisis every time I had a moment of success, I'd have to choose relationships wisely. I'd have to be clear right at the outset, at base camp, about what meant the most to me and how I could also be that for others.

I wanted friendships that didn't require a birthday or an event to see each other, where it was Tuesday and that was reason enough to get together and belly laugh and get deep if we needed to. I wanted friends whom I could trust with my thoughts. Understanding the traits we want in our friendships helps us explore what to look for and also how we may need to show up as well. I remember my mom telling me, "Don't only put value into the people you're dating. Those relationships are important, but your most important relationships will be your friendships. When everything goes down, they will be the ones who are there for you." This is truth. Having community is abundance. It's worth more than gold.

I wanted "one precious life" to be an affirmation, not just a quote that I'd read and carried within me. This voyage of building and maintaining a life that felt and mirrored peace started with my relationships. And it would uncover things as I walked, as healing always does. Through the perspective of my life being a precious thing, I had a different point of view. When we treat something like it's precious, we handle it with care. We'd bubble-wrap it if we were concerned about a potential fall. We'd prioritize its needs. And we'd want people around who validated that we were vulnerable too. We'd want people who conceded to our softness. We'd see that others were just as precious as we were. We'd treat each other as such.

But we're not the fine china that you keep in the glass cabinet that no one can touch or have access to. The word *wild* is boisterous. Your life can be bold, vivid, riveting, and beguiling. To be precious and to be wild. To have relationships where both can exist. Where all of you can exist. Life can be rocky and unpredictable. Fine china was not what I wanted to bring with me on this journey. I needed something that wasn't so fragile.

I thought looking at my friendships would be a gentle sashay through fields filled with flowers and fruitful trees. I only expected to find beauty because I ignored what was rotting. I wasn't looking around at this garden of relationships with honest eyes. "Everything is fine in my friendships," I naively said to myself. Yes, there was light all around me in this beautiful space, but there was also shade.

While looking into friendships, I noticed that most people fell into a few groups:

- People I don't know in real life, we've only chatted online.
  These are people we're friendly with.
- People I don't know well, but I like.
  These are people we may develop friendships with.
- People I know well, and who don't treat me well, but I like.
  These are relationships we need to end.
- People I know well, but it's only professional.
  These can be friendly, but these are not friendships.
- People I know well, who treat me well, and the relationship is mutual.
  These are our friends. **These are our people.**

When you look at these categories, where do your friends fit? Take some time and write down which category your relationships are in; it's bound to give you clarity. Are there people whom you consider to be friends who don't respect you? Are there people you consider to be your friends who aren't invested in the relationship in the same way you are? I immediately knew who the people were who weren't treating me well. I was surprised by how quickly I knew because I thought to myself, "If I know this, why are they still here?" They were still in my life because I'd swept many of them into the category "that's just how they are." This phrase is like shining a light in someone's eyes; it blinds you from seeing things clearly. If this was "just how they were," then their behavior wasn't mean, it was *their personality*. Instead of being honest with myself about their harmful behavior, I excused their comments or conduct as a personality trait. Excusing their behavior was draining me. It drains all of us.

My phone would buzz, and I'd check the screen to see who it was. Depending on the name, I felt either excitement to chat or instant anxiety about what to do. Even when we ignore harm, our bodies always respond to what's happening around us. I'd worry and go back and forth on whether I should pick up, knowing that this conversation would most likely shift my energy, ruining the rest of my afternoon. Or should I ignore the call, knowing that I'd feel the same anxiety about what they were going to say to me later about not answering? This was before I had boundaries. This was before I understood what healthy relationships looked like. At base camp, I got clear on what friendship meant to me and why I was saying yes to someone being in my life. I desired a high-vibrational life, but it would require me to choose people and surroundings that matched. It would require me to be a match as well. This work is laying the blueprint for the friendships you'll have in the future. You can revisit these routes you took toward healthy relationships, to continue to build a community that walks alongside you with love.

INTENT

Friendship is such an important part of who we are and our feeling of joy in the world. I don't believe we do life well without quality friends around us. I delightfully discovered that I had a few, and I knew life would be so much tougher without them. Creating friendships is crucial to our well-being. We need connection and supportive people around us, and having this in our lives helps us feel less alone. Knowing that we can be who we are with the people we love and that we're accepted, seen, and valued is priceless. The other side of this is losing friendships. I remember realizing that a friendship I thought I'd have forever was ending. It was painful and I swore that I would never go through it again, but it wasn't the last time that a relationship had run its course in my life. The relationships that end aren't always because of some big drama. Sometimes we slowly drift apart. Perhaps you're doing the painful work of realizing a friendship is no longer serving you, or that it has simply run its course. If this is you, you're not alone. It can be scary to put yourself out there again. It can be scary to take the risk. But we need friends. We need community, and it's an integral part of our feeling grounded, secure, and joyful in our lives. Do you feel you're missing friends and community in your life? Are you surrounded by filler friends on whom you've spent so much of your energy that you don't realize you're energetically depleted?

There's been a lot of societal chatter about "no new friends," which is the idea of not making any new friends and sticking solely with the folks you've known the longest. For some people this might be great if they have a solid group of people in their lives that feels healthy and supportive. But for others, it keeps you stuck in crappy relationships that need to end. Despite knowing that I had a few relationships that fell into the latter category, part of me understood this mantra of not putting yourself out there. People are tired of the drama that can come with any relationship, let alone new relationships with new needs and new feelings. People are tired of making themselves emotionally available, only to be met with lack. People are tired of being disappointed by folks who seem to want to be friends but never show up. I was also "people" sometimes, terrified of letting people in. But this mantra didn't feel true enough to stand in. I knew I had a choice, and I knew the people I had around me were an important part of my well-being. You also have a choice to not give up on friendship just because there've been people who weren't for you. Your people exist!

Michelle Obama talks about her "kitchen table" of friends. She shared, "When I became First Lady of the United States, I realized I have a choice. I can either close up, no new friends, or I can find a way that, even in this odd position, to reach out and find new people in my life." Closing up is often something we want to do out of fear. But she calls her "kitchen table" a place to gather new friends and old. And taking the step to bring people in enriches our lives.

This part of your map will lead you to the type of people you want in your life. What kinds of journeys do you want to go on with your friends? What kind of person would be interested in the paths you're already on? Who are the people who will walk the tough paths with you? We don't have to have the exact same interests; even identical twins are individual. But we *do* want people who like what we like and vice versa. This helps us get out of the mentality of trying to make things work with people who don't want it to work with us. Find people who do. Find people who believe you are an immediate yes.

Once you get clear on what you desire for your friendships, the people who don't fall into the friend category will become even clearer. I was giving the title "friend" away too haphazardly. I love how I show up for people I care about. But because I spoke of these folks as friends, I ignored their unkindness, lack of commitment, and toxicity. I treated them as friends because I chose to believe the words coming out of their mouths rather than accepting their actions. I was showing up with pure intentions and I automatically believed they were too. That's not how life works.

Tyler Perry has an analogy on friends that shook me to my core. He shares that leaf people aren't going to be around long-term. These people come and go without investment in the relationship. Branch people may appear to be committed to the friendship, but their consistency may still waver. Most likely they won't be around for the long haul either. But root people, *"like the roots of a tree, they are hard to find because they are not trying to be seen. Their only job is to hold you up and help you live a strong and healthy life. . . . **And if you go through an awful storm, they will hold you up.**"*

When I read the "root friends" section, I knew that this was my intention for my relationships. And after spending time holding space for friends and clients in my workshops and courses, I know this is what most people want too. We don't just want this from our friends; we want to be root people for others too. We want to send flowers to friends, letting them know we care. We want to send notes of affirmation when our friends need them. We *want* to be there in the relationships that feel safe and solid enough to do so. There isn't a more powerful path that we can walk than learning who our people are. They help make every step we take richer.

As I continued to stride down my path of friendships, I could feel the aloneness I'd been ignoring. I couldn't lie to myself anymore, and I'd gotten so good at lying to myself. I was able to swallow cries without anyone noticing, hiding my emotions because they weren't safe with all the people I was spending time with. But I couldn't ignore the mirror any longer. It was time to witness myself upholding relationships that stood on mountains of lies and discomfort. I trudged through the many, many cancellations from people who'd discard our plans without care or rescheduling. I paid attention to the lack of smiles when I was celebrating. I looked at the way I treated them versus their actions toward me. When you look at your relationships for what they are, you may be tempted to tell your so-called friends about themselves. Once you see the truth, it's deliciously seductive to go off on them, I know. But you don't need to dedicate any more energy to people you're not a priority to. There will be relationships that can be salvaged. But you already know which ones those are. See the truth and free yourself. No more lies. No more energetic entanglements.

And just as I said *no more lies* to myself, the ground beneath me collapsed and I fell through the layers below the earth I was just standing on. In what felt like moments, once again my focus flipped from the people I did have in my life to the people who weren't good for me whom I released, and it took over my energy. I was lower than low. No one ever talks about how choosing yourself can almost crush you. Although it is the thing we must do, the very choice that empowers us to stand, we often have to step over versions of us that we loved, people we thought loved us, and dreams that will never be fulfilled to get to solid ground. That moment of witnessing the truth can warp your mind and make you believe, if *they* don't care about me, then *no one* cares about me. I'd go online and endlessly scroll, no matter how much it hurt me. Have you ever gone on social media and been met by a sea of smiling faces and wondered, were they as happy as they appeared to be? Was I the only one feeling this loneliness? I watched people with their friends on vacation, enjoying one another's company, even matching outfits. I saw the birthday trib-ute posts and the dinners they were having in the evening to celebrate. I saw the easy evenings of having a drink together on someone's patio. People in community together. Or what I believed was community.

Social media will fool you into believing that because you don't have a color-coordinated surprise party that ends on a yacht, you don't have friends who *care about you*. Social media can distract you from solving your loneliness through con-necting with people in real life, and instead force you to fall deeper into self-loathing about what you feel you're missing that you believe someone else has. Myleik Teele's quote "You think you want what someone has, but what you really want is how you think it makes them feel" is the experience of what's happening to so many of us stuck in voyeurism. Comparison is a trickster, and it doesn't have to win. We want relationships that anchor us. Connectedness. Connectedness comes from leaning in.

But sometimes the illumination of truth gets too heavy. Looking in the mirror, acknowledging the shade, and being honest highlighted all the problems that were already there, the ones I ignored to spare my feelings. Once I shined a light on them, I couldn't escape the clouds overhead. Once I shined a light on how some people in my life didn't value me, every-thing got darker.

WALK THE TALK

When you fall in a deep hole, you're so startled by the drop that you need a minute to gather yourself. You never think to look around. You aren't thinking about anything other than the light that you're looking up at from the place you fell, the hole of light that now seems so far away. It feels like you'll never reach it. You may jump and try to get back up to it, but it's clear you can't get out of the dark the same way you came in. I found myself foraging through this dark space, picking feeling after feeling and trying to identify which ones were which, and I learned so much.

Some of our devastation comes from the amount of time and energy we poured into relationships when we could've used it on so many other things. We're pissed that we didn't recognize the signs, and if we did, we're saddened by the fact that we didn't act on them sooner. Unhealthy relationships sometimes give us physical signs that they're not working for us through the experience of nausea, anxiety, or a feeling of sickness. The Whitehall II study shows that negative close relationships produce a higher risk of coronary events. Who we have around us is critical to our overall well-being. Our friendships can improve our lives or drain us. We must choose friends like we care about ourselves too.

On the other hand, loneliness is a major health issue. The

US surgeon general called attention to the "public health crisis on loneliness, isolation, and lack of connection in our country," stating: "loneliness and isolation increase the risk for individuals to develop mental health challenges in their lives, and lacking connection can increase the risk for premature death to levels comparable to smoking daily." Some of us are keeping people around us because we don't want to feel any lonelier than we already do. Because when you feel lonely in a crowd of "friends," you fear that the one or two good people whom you have around you won't be enough. I remember keeping those filler friends because if I let them go, then what would I do? Would I just hang with the couple of folks who were solid? And the answer is *yes*. We say yes to living our lives with less drama and more connection with the people who are showing up. We release the noise, the stress, the pushing, and the pulling. Sometimes we are the lead actors in our own dramas. It's time to let all that go.

As I looked around that dark, cold hole that I'd fallen in, it didn't look familiar. From what I could make of it, I knew I'd never seen these surroundings, even though my eyes were still adjusting. But it *felt* familiar. It was déjà vu. I knew that I'd walked through these emotions at another time in my life. I took a seat in my hole because there wasn't much else I could do at that point. I was tired from all the self-awareness. This work can be exhausting at times. As I sat there, I focused on my leaf people. The folks who were always too busy to show up when I needed them but would take and take and take. It's not that they didn't care about me. I couldn't prove that, so I didn't want to fixate on it. The thought that "nobody cared" was what got me in this hole in the first place, and I knew that story wasn't true. People *did* care about me. The narrative that "no one cared" was causing me to focus on the lack instead of the abundant people I had in my life. This happens to so many of us. Yes, it was sad to know that I kept pouring myself into people who maybe didn't care about what I was going through. But we can choose to pour ourselves elsewhere. We don't have to keep trying to repair those broken connections. Remind yourself of the beauty that you offer this world. Who they were to you as a *friend* isn't because of any flaws you have. You matter even if you weren't a priority to them. **I want you to remember that you matter.**

And then I remembered why this hole I was in felt familiar. Eventually, I got brave enough to look around that dark hole I'd fallen in. Now, with eyes adjusted to the darkness, what once felt scary to look at didn't feel so overwhelming anymore. The magical thing about darkness underground is that it's where the roots live. Even if I was untouchable by others, my root people could easily get to me. While courageously looking around, I saw that I was standing on solid ground, I was still on my path. I was fooled into believing that I was derailed by my fall, but this was merely a stopping point. A gathering place. A reconnection portal with myself and the people who really mattered to me. The people who'd always been there, who I couldn't see or hear with all the noise around. The people who wanted me to see me the way they saw me, wild and precious. And free. They held me and walked me back to the light. Reminding me that anytime I fell, they'd be there. And that's what your root people can be for you too.

It was heavy. It was also liberating. I struggled with knowing that I felt so poorly about myself. When people treat us badly, we might believe it's because we deserve it even though we know it's wrong. Friendships with people who see the light in you and are willing to help you shine brightly again are a blessing. Just having one person in your life willing to help you remember who you are when you get lost is everything. Because when you can't remember the route on your map, they can help you find your way out.

If you're still building your community of root people, remember that learning to make friends is not a flaw. Your humanness is not evidence of fraudulence. That's perfectionism talking and saying that you should know everything, when in fact being human means that we're all constantly learning. It's hard to believe that learning is okay when we watch people being constantly praised and accepted for their expertise or how amazing their life appears to be. Even those people are learning. Allow these lessons to reroute you when you find you're no longer where you want to be.

My root friends were ready to walk with me. And we need them. They help make the journey more easeful. They are the mirrors we can look to, reflecting the truth of who we are. Now safely escorted by my root friends, I could see there was a multitude of pathways that I could choose to lead me to my peace and I only had one question to answer: Which way did I want to go?

LESSONS LEARNED

I was at a book event in DC, celebrating the launch of Rachel Cargle's first book, *A Renaissance of Our Own*. Her moderator, my friend the author Glory Edim, the founder of Well-Read Black Girl, asked Rachel what brought about the pivot she'd made in her business recently. Rachel, a philanthropist and activist among many other titles, had changed her online presence from being a place to come and learn about the devastating reality of racism and violence, to the place where you'd come to see the beauty of Blackness in absolute abundance, literally pushing against every oppressive tactic . . . simply by living fully. There was grief, there was art, there was joy, and there was softness. I remember witnessing this shift myself, and I was enamored. The boldness to pivot with no explanation. To change paths and walk proudly was inspiring. Rachel replied to Glory's question, saying, "I want to experience joy in living and show others what liberation can look like. I don't know what's on the other side of right now, so I want to enjoy." She also talked about her desire to really love her friends and community. She often shares a reminder to her community on Fridays to show up for a friend in their life, maybe to buy them a coffee or send a note of affirmation, to remind them that they care. This very simple but powerful way of showing up is possible only when we're present.

The goal isn't to be absorbed by the fear of what might come in our relationships, refusing to put ourselves out there because of the potential mishaps. Things will go wrong sometimes. There will be misunderstandings. There may be fights. There may be times when the people you love disappoint you and moments when you disappoint them. Peace is not perfection. Love is not perfection. The goal is to remain fixed on love amid what could come our way.

Peace requires presence. Truth requires presence. Peace is not lazy, but peace is a place of rest. Peace requires our full commitment. It needs us to show up and defy the reality around us if what surrounds us isn't aligned. If you want fulfilling relationships, you need to energetically match that energy within yourself. Are you as committed to the people you have relationships with as they are to you? Are you prioritizing your relationships in the same way you'd like them to? Are you able to communicate your needs while also being a resting place for the needs of others? How are you spending your time? Who is allowed access to you and why? Do the people around you embody the essence of peace as you define it?

My scarcity mindset came from feeling alone from as early as I could remember. Even though I had loving people in my life, I didn't believe I was enough. I traded my worth for a bunch of filler people. This didn't make them bad people. This didn't make me a bad person either. I was lost on my path, and it took me falling into a hole to let my people guide me on my way again.

I could count on one hand how many root people are in my life, and I wouldn't even use all my fingers. But their roots are so stable and substantive that I am filled. Do they always show up the way that I want them to? No, root people are still human, but their love never ends. Am I still forging other friendships? Absolutely, there's too many wonderful people out there to not!

I still wasn't in New York City, the place I'd mistakenly believed was the only space I would be held. This false belief had kept me from fully rooting in the home that lived within me. I learned a lot by falling into that hole. There were times I thought I wouldn't make it out, and that instead of basking in the light, I'd be surrounded by shadows and only have memories of what happiness used to feel like. I had to surrender to the support around me, and sometimes I had to trust their reflections of me, because when I saw myself, I saw the worst. I had to learn compassion for myself. I had to learn to let compassion in from the people around me, my root people. And as hard as this was, it took away the naivety I'd had about relationships.

The same way that unhealthy relationships can impact our well-being, healthy ones can too. Our friends are our companions on the journey. They are the best parts of us, and they are willing to be with us when the worst shows up. Your friends want to hold you up. They relish your accomplishments as if they're happening to them, because your happiness means that much. They hold you with steady consistency when you're alone. But your friends can't force you to see them. They can't force you to place your energies with them. It's up to you to notice where the roots run deep. Go there. That's where you'll find your abundant garden with flowers and fruit trees. Here is where there's anchoring. Here is where we thrive.

6

JOY IN ALL OF
THE PEOPLE
I AM:
ON SAYING
YES TO JOY

I was finally going to see Elton John. I'd loved his music, and really all music, my whole life. When things were going good at home growing up, we'd play music loudly and dance, and there was so much joy in those moments. When things weren't going well, I'd play music to try to escape—an attempt to return to moments of joy. I had no idea that the journey of going to this concert would unlock so many truths in me.

I'd never made it to one of his concerts, and as I thought about my wish to go, I felt a familiar immediate response of *no* that came in before I even had the chance to investigate it. It became clear to me that this no was preventing me from going to many events, despite how much they contributed to my joy. I believe this was my body's way of preventing disappointment. I'd say no to myself before I had the chance to hear the no's from the people I'd ask to come with me. But this time was different; this was Elton's "goodbye tour," which meant this was probably the last chance I'd get to see him. So instead of listening to the no, I set off to try to make this one work.

But in familiar fashion, as I checked in with friends, either folks didn't want to go or they couldn't go during the time that he was having his concerts in the States. And then I thought about it. What if I went to see him in London? A friend and I tried to make it work, but it just wasn't going to fit our schedules. So I scrapped the whole idea and moved from excitement to frustration. Frustration with myself.

What was stopping me from going to this concert alone, I thought to myself. "Ummm . . . fear?" my inner thoughts quickly replied. I was afraid. I'd traveled alone many times, but it was always for work. I'd been doing some form of travel for work since I was fifteen years old, whether by train or plane, and that kind of solo travel felt doable. It felt less self-important. I *had* to travel for work, so if I happened to enjoy myself while there, it wasn't because I'd just gone on vacation to have a good time. That felt acceptable. But traveling just for me? Would I really take time off to travel for a concert and build a whole trip around it?

None of this was really about Elton John, or my love of music. This was about questioning my beliefs around joy and whether I was willing to go for it alone. This was also about questioning my beliefs about what I deserved and unlearning the unhealthy rules I'd placed on myself around fun. And yes, we want people to come with us on our adventures. We've talked about the importance of having our root friends and people who will be there for us, but everyone is still living their own lives and has their own interests, no matter how much they care about us. And so do we. Am I willing to do the things that I want to do, with or without anyone? Are you? Am I willing to take the leap and enjoy myself, no reasons required? Are you?

I went back to that statement my grandmother said to me that I shared earlier: "You have done so much in your short life. I love that about you." I always replayed this when I was about to walk away from something I wanted out of fear. How often do we say no to what we wish for and list off all the reasons . . . ahem, excuses . . . for why we shouldn't go for it?

We sing YOLO at the top of our lungs, and yet we commit to living in confinement, watching other people live their lives on TV or from our phones, wishing we had the opportunity to do what we want too. But we do. We may not be able to do what we fully dream yet—for example, I won't be spending three months in Europe anytime soon (I don't think so anyway)—but we can step toward it. We forget that this big, beautiful path that we're on can lead wherever we want it to! We're allowed to take moments where we are and enjoy them. And I'd never done that before. I decided it was time.

BASE CAMP

Let's be real: As exciting as this felt, it was a big deal for me. And as I talked to friends about what I was planning, I realized it was a big deal for most. This *still* meant traveling by myself (with no one meeting me there like on a work trip), dining by myself, walking around a city by myself, and going to a concert solo. Was I ready for my *Eat, Pray, Love* moment? As I hear myself say this, I'm cringing at me thinking twice about taking time for myself, even if it was solo. But I know I'm not the only one who has felt these same feelings before, deciding that what I want for myself is perhaps too much. So, before I could talk myself out of it, I bought the concert ticket and the plane ticket. I took a deep breath. And I started my walk.

For the first time, I was planning something that was purely pleasure for me. This wasn't a party for my family or an event that other people would take part in. It was just for me, and throughout most of my adult life, I didn't make a lot of space for myself. I know I'm not alone in this. You might find that you often prioritize everyone else over yourself as well. And that you haven't had space to do something just for you. Or maybe you haven't felt you had the permission to do you. Whether I was spending time in an unhealthy partnership or fretting about someone else's situation, I spent a lot of my energy on stuff that wasn't mine. So this was exhilarating. Just preparing for the trip unlocked beliefs that I was carrying that I wanted to release. I kept thinking, "This is what freedom feels like." I also made a note that I wanted to feel this feeling more, and not just when I was going on a trip. This was a significant moment. I was rewriting the "rules" of what's acceptable for me as a woman, a mom, or any of the titles I wore.

I was hopefully making it clear what was possible for the generations coming behind me too.

Hopefully my daughters looked at me and didn't feel doom about what was coming in adulthood, but excitement about what they could create. Hopefully, by choosing to live my life for myself, they'd see that taking time for yourself did take intention, but helped you design a life that was yours. Really yours. A life where you weren't just doing what you'd seen done before you. A life where you could follow the blueprint if you wanted to or where you could choose to scrap it completely and instead do what feels good to you. It did take work, and also as a mom of two, having a supportive partner was incredibly helpful. But it was not only possible to make space for myself, this step improved my sense of self. And the better we feel about ourselves, the better we show up for the people we love.

No one wants to sound insufferable. There's a voice that many of us have within that tells us to shut up when we feel like we're taking up too much space. Sharing about the fear of planning a solo trip not only felt incredibly privileged (and it was) but also unimportant. I know there will be people who read this chapter and roll their eyes. And I also know that there will be people who read this chapter who've also felt the same desire to shrink in the face of others' judgments. Dr. Brené Brown shares, "Comparative suffering is a function of fear and scarcity. . . . If there's one thing I've learned over the past decade, it's that fear and scarcity immediately trigger comparison, and even pain and hurt are not immune to being assessed and ranked. . . . I'm not allowed to feel disappointed about being passed over for promotion when my friend just found out that his wife has cancer. You're feeling shame for forgetting your son's school play? Please—that's a first-world problem; there are people dying of starvation every minute." We measure ourselves against the world and invalidate our own feelings. And this leads to shame and a sense of being alone in our challenges.

This doesn't mean that we invalidate the very real and serious problems that others are facing. It means we can show up for them with empathy while showing up for ourselves with empathy too. This felt important to share before I asked if you could relate to struggling with time for yourself, because when I ask clients this question, they often list the reasons why what they're experiencing isn't that big of a deal. And if it matters to you, it matters.

As the trip got nearer, I started thinking about all the things I wanted to do the last time I was in England that I didn't get a chance to do while there with my husband. To be clear, he is my favorite person to travel with. We have a very similar vibe when it comes to vacationing. But there are some things that I want to see and do, like visit Downton Abbey (aka Highclere Castle), for example, that he could go without. And I noticed how on trips with friends or my partner, so much of what I wanted was put on the back burner. And probably the same for them too. Most of our lives are spent compromising, and as we grow, we realize that we don't often spend time doing just what we want to do. There's nothing wrong with compromise;

it's an essential attribute of healthy relationships. But when do we get to just be ourselves? I wanted to change that. We hold resentment, whether we want to admit it or not, when we don't allow ourselves to *be*. I didn't want to plan to live my life only after my kids grew up; I wanted them to witness me taking care of them *and* living for me too right now.

I opened a whole new world for myself. I started wondering about how much of my everyday life was me putting me on hold because I wasn't giving myself permission to do things I wanted without others. Why wasn't I dining alone at the restaurants I wanted to try? Why wasn't I going to the arts festival I was excited about? Why wasn't I going to learn more at the exhibitions that focused on my interests by myself? Why was I talking about what I *would* be able to do if people wanted to do it with me, *rather than just doing it myself*? PS: A lot of my friendship stuff from the other chapter wouldn't have existed if I'd known the importance of setting off on my own sometimes. We don't need to keep people around just for the sake of having someone to do things with, especially when they are harmful. We don't need to persuade or coerce people to do things that they don't want to do in the name of friendship. Enjoying your own company is healing. Enjoying your own company doing the things you love? Now, that's joy.

INTENT

When I teach about incorporating joy in your daily life in my workshops, I'm always met with a barrage of statements that can be summarized by saying the words *we don't have the time.* People always give me the side-eye at how joy is very nice, but also not on their priority list of things to achieve daily. Maybe they'll get around to joy on the weekend, if all their laundry is done.

And I think about this often, especially when I find that I've gotten in an adulting loop that's missing regular moments of joy. One of the reasons I took the leap to start my own business was because I didn't want a life that was fully dictated by work. At my last nine-to-five job, I'd spent years talking my boss into remote work, and then I finally got it. And it was through that experience I learned that working remotely still didn't give me enough time for me. Even though I didn't have to get up and go into the office, I was still stuck to a computer for nine or ten hours a day. There was no time to do the things I wanted, like writing this book. This is what I think people are talking about when they say they're lacking time.

The truth is that every job isn't going to be able to be done from your computer at home. Some folks are working multiple jobs. Others are in school and working. And others don't have a traditional nine-to-five, but they take care of their families full-time, and that job also takes up so much time. So when do we get to take care of us? How can we fit ourselves in?

I think it's important to define what joy means for you. For a friend of mine, joy is being able to see the water from her house. After her long commute, when she comes home and sees the water from her beautiful patio, she feels immense joy. That's a version of joy that she can access every day. Does listening to a comedy podcast bring you joy? Does having a cup of tea while reading a magazine bring you joy? Yes, we want big, unbridled joy. That's what this trip felt like for me. But when the trip is over or if the trip doesn't come again for some time, where can I experience joy daily? This was another intention that I was excited to explore on this journey.

A week before the trip, I started getting scared to do this eleven-day adventure alone. I even checked in with a few friends to see if they would be able to fly out during parts of my trip to meet me last-minute. Everyone was down, but no one could make it work. "Dammit, I'm really going through with this by myself."

On the night that I flew out, as I walked through a deserted Dulles Airport, I didn't feel the way I thought I would. The fear had been replaced by something else. Independence? I hadn't even stepped foot on the plane yet and I felt liberated. Partly because I knew the next eleven days were mine. I owned my time right now. But also because I was doing the things. I had a habit of talking about things that I always wanted to do that didn't concern my career, and never planning to do them. I'd think about the list of what I wanted sometimes, and I'd feel down about not having checked anything off. Over time, I realized that many of the things I'd written down were doable, I just wasn't taking any action toward them. Today, I wasn't just talking about doing them one day. This felt big. What are the things that you talk about doing that you've never acted on? How can you start small today?

When I arrived in London, I still remembered my way around Heathrow Airport from my last time. However, this was my first time taking the tube and the Bath line on the GWR, and it was a legit nightmare trying to figure it all out. A nightmare that was a lot of fun. I ran from train to train, realizing that I'd booked the two trains way too close together for someone who had no idea where they were going. Luckily, I made both just in time. I chatted with people who helped me find my way around, something I don't often do when I'm traveling alone near home, because I'm usually in cities where I know where I'm going or I'm in a cab. I even met a lovely woman whom I asked for directions when I was lost at the Bath train station. In typical raining-out-of-nowhere UK fashion, I went to open my umbrella and it broke in half the moment I pulled it open. A passerby smiled at me with a face that said "That's life sometimes, right?" Indeed. I threw the umbrella out and, in that moment, it really began to pour. Putting my hood up, I walked over to this woman to ask for directions, as I really didn't want to continue going the wrong way. In the pouring British rain, she insisted on walking me to my hotel under her umbrella, while telling me all the best spots to eat. I took her advice and went to the best spots to eat and while there I met other travelers and locals. We chatted and caught up on everything happening in our lives, as if we were friends who hadn't seen one another in years.

I was missing this in my life. The spontaneity. The meetups with strangers that were lovely but were only for this evening, or perhaps a moment, and then we'd set each other free, wishing the best of luck on our paths. It was wonderful.

WALK THE TALK

Audre Lorde has a beautiful quote that states, "I am still learning how to take joy in all the people I am, how to use all my selves in the service of what I believe, how to accept when I fail and rejoice when I succeed." This spoke to me. Meeting new people is vulnerable. Telling parts of your story, witnessing their truths, and finding things that you both relate on is liberating. Through others, we're reminded that we aren't so different from anyone. Meeting new people was encouraging me to release old stories about versions of who I was that were filled with tales of how joy needed to look. Joy is a chameleon. It can fit wherever and however we need it to, if we're willing to allow it.

It's brave to accept joy despite shame reminding you of all the times that you've rejected it. Shame loves to remind us of moments when we said no to ourselves. It finds us on our paths of light and questions whether we truly believe we deserve to be there. Shame loves to tell us that we are compromised and unable to experience the level of joy we seek. Shame is wrong.

I could see that on the different paths I'd taken, joy was confined to very specific circumstances. Some versions of me were allowed to have joy and other parts of me were sheltered from it. Shame was asking me, "Do you really love *all* the versions of you that came before this? Did those versions *really* help you get here?" Shame was asking me the questions that *it knew* could make me think that I didn't deserve this time and space. That I didn't deserve this joy, or these connections, or this trip. Old stories like to come up and wave their unwelcome hands to distract us from the freedom we've created. And mine wanted to remind me of the moments when I didn't make the right decisions, or perhaps I didn't show up as my best self. Shame wanted to know, did joy exist in all of those versions of me too? It surely didn't always feel like it. But shame wasn't going to win this fight, not this time. We have to be willing to look shame in the face and give it what it needs. Loving truth.

I noticed that since I was in a state of joy while contemplating all of this, shame had less strength than it normally had. Shame didn't seem as loud. Joy was a friend in this fight as shame kept egging me on, asking, "Did joy *really* exist in the version of you who stayed with the boyfriend who made you sit in the back seat of his car while his friend rode in the front, and yet you complied and did it?" Did joy really live in the versions of me that I can't bear to look at or speak of because I'm embarrassed I didn't say yes to me? Could there be beauty in the parts of our lives that weren't *great*? Shame was trying to separate me from my joy. But I knew that joy was part of me. I could feel it.

This trip was teaching me that when we return to self, we return to joy. Joy never leaves us; it's always there waiting for us to say yes. Even though joy can sometimes feel far away, it's always within us. We can always find our way back to it. And for the first time in a long while, I was giving myself permission to be immersed in it. Recognizing that I didn't have to leave joy ever again. Remember that joy is in all of us. It remains even when we betray ourselves, it remains even when we unintentionally hurt someone, it remains even when we're passive-aggressive and have to apologize for our actions. It's even there when it feels like everything is falling apart. We don't have to turn over our joy because we have human experiences.

You don't have to explain why you didn't choose joy before. You don't have to get caught up in all the things you "should've" done that would've given you something different. You can stand proudly with all the different versions of yourself who tried their hardest to create the best life. And thank goodness the definition of a good life keeps transforming, because as you grow you'll witness new versions of you that you weren't sure you could evolve into. Shame couldn't win this time because joy helped take the walls down. And when the walls are down, you can see. You can feel. All those stories that you tell yourself aren't true. We deserve it all.

How many times have you told yourself that there was one part of you that was exempt from joy? That all the other parts of you were allowed to participate, but that this one part (or parts) had to stay silent and commit to life without radiance? That this part of you had done something so bad or had messed up so much that it had to stay in the shadows? I want us to get curious about this. I am certain that the way we feel about ourselves and whether we believe we are deserving of joy impacts the way we treat ourselves. And it impacts the way we're able to be there for ourselves.

On my trip, I noticed how I really cared for myself, taking all my physical and emotional feelings into consideration, even when they felt small. I sat on a bench in St. James's Park when I was a bit tired from a long walk instead of pushing myself to finish. I didn't set alarms and scheduled my whole day around waking up when my body needed to. I walked everywhere, no matter how much time it was going to take, because I was craving the movement. This was me learning to integrate joy into all the people I am by loving me today. We don't have to live in the shadows. It's safe to live and be who we are out loud.

I remember watching my grandmother and seeing the immense light that always seemed to live within her. I honestly couldn't believe the way she was always connected to joy despite what she was going through. She wasn't experiencing joy from a place of ignorance or lack of awareness of her circumstances. No, I think she chose joy despite the tough parts that existed. She was carrying her joy with her, no matter what path she was on.

This became my goal. I want joy to accompany me wherever I go. I want to remember that joy is with me always. We are joy embodied. This trip was awakening the joy in me that was dormant but still as vibrant as if it never went away. And I know it can be tough to believe in joy's presence when it gets dark. I also understand that our everyday lives require a lot more structure and it can feel tough to fit unscheduled joy in. I know my priorities shift when I'm home and I have to be more intentional about my time. But, outside of my priorities, what are the messages that I'm telling all the selves who have brought me to where I am today? What do you tell yourself?

LESSONS LEARNED

I was learning to welcome joy like a friend. I'd already made good friends with pain and grief, but joy, consistent and long-lasting joy, was new, and I liked it. Earlier I talked about the fears that would come up when abundance came near, and the thoughts I had about what I might have to give up to receive it fully. We watch others in their abundance and feel so triggered by their ability to make it look easy. I know I've been there. I'm sure you have too. What would the universe want from me in return? I'd always shudder and think whenever opportunity came. So many of us are nervous to welcome in the good because we don't know if we're welcoming in the bad too. The wheat and the weeds both ready for harvest.

This was such a complete waste of my time. It wastes all our time. We aren't any more prepared when we spend our energy waiting for the ball to drop. We aren't any more ready for disaster when we've spent years and years worrying. If something causes discomfort, let's get used to looking at it, talking about it, and figuring out what we need to do to live with it or release it. Or perhaps the discomfort is an invitation to live without it. Whatever we choose, joy can be in those conversations too. A friend on the journey. This is the other side.

It was the night of the concert. I was so excited, and it felt surreal to be there. When I got to my seat, my seatmate was already there with her husband. We smiled at each other as I sat down, and we began talking instantly. She was from Wales and would be visiting New York soon because it was on her bucket list to do before turning fifty. I asked her all about Wales and where to visit, as it was on my list too. We talked about rose-colored glasses; we laughed over our drinks. And when the music started, we sang songs and looked at each other in disbelief that this concert was this good. That life could be this good.

By now we know this isn't about Elton, right? Really, the magic of this concert could stand alone, but it was amplified by experiencing what life was like when I decided to step out of my comfort zone. I was by myself, but I wasn't alone. I think that as a woman I'd fallen into the societal ideals of doing things with friends or a partner, or something that was solely for my kids. As much as I tried to remain me among all the other ways that I show up in the world, that part of me, myself, was evaporated, and it hurt me that this part of me felt like the past.

The hurt was showing up in my short responses to simple questions from my husband. The hurt was showing up in crying spells on Monday when I realized the week was jam-packed with work and school activities too, and I *knew* that having time for me was going to be impossible. The hurt was showing up when I started dreading work, the thing I love doing, because I realized that I was either working for my business or working as a family member, and that I was exhausted. For joy to exist, we must first be willing to admit its absence. That day after day, when we called out to joy to see if there was space for it to show up, it was consistently marked absent. The lives we designed weren't compatible with it. But this could change. We have the power to do it.

It may seem like it took me removing myself from the life I'd built to be able to see what it really was. The beauty, the monotonous moments, all of it. When we feel like life is a repetitious Groundhog Day, our joy can feel far away. It can also feel like we're watching our lives go by, versus actively living. When it feels like all we do is *get up, go to work, eat an "okay" lunch, go back to work, commute home, get home and have dinner, clean, maybe get your dog out, maybe pay a bill, shower, watch the TV show you've been looking forward to all day, only to wake up at 2 a.m. to an incredibly loud infomercial because you fell asleep during your favorite show and you have to get up in three hours or so and do it all again*, it's heavy. Wash, rinse, repeat. The sameness of life can feel suffocating. It stifles joy and makes it feel distant. But the truth is, I'd realized these discomforts and feelings long before this eleven-day trip. I just didn't decide to do anything about it. Booking that ticket forced me to make changes. But we don't have to go on trips to shift our lives. That's not always feasible or realistic.

Now that I was back from London, it was time to take a good look at my life. What was my schedule? When was I waking up and was this time working for me? When were the best times to take time for me? Things are changing in my life all the time, and I noticed that instead of stopping to ask myself what I needed, I'd been running behind my life just trying to keep up.

Have you ever been in this position? Where your path is throwing you so many curves, even if they're positive, that you can't keep up, so you feel like you're trailing behind? The thing is, we're still in command. No matter how much we feel like life is the one telling us what to do, we're still the ones who decide how it plays out on our road. It can be easy to feel like a casualty to life's plans. Like our dreams were just meaningless affirmations and reality is something far different. I was recently asked the question "Aren't affirmations just an example of lying to yourself?" It can feel like that when your life feels so drastically different from what you desire. And listen, I know it can be tough to be in an apartment dreaming about the yacht life. Those two images can feel very far apart. But what I shared in response to this question is that affirmations aren't the absence of reality. Affirmations give us an opportunity to SAY OUT LOUD the things that we're often too afraid to admit we want. We keep so much inside, and we trudge along. We do it because we're tired. We do it because we don't want to hear negative comments from others. And we do it because we don't know what else to do. PS: We also often dream of the grandiose because we feel that it's the only way we can access joy. But wealth comes in many forms. What does a supported, loving, free life feel like to you?

This whole trip, this whole experience, this whole moment started with an affirmation. I wrote down that I wanted to travel more and do things that I'd always dreamed of. I wrote down the places I wanted to go. I wrote down the things I wanted to experience. I wrote them down years before I had the means to do it. I didn't know when they'd happen. I didn't know how they'd come to be. But I believed and walked toward them.

When it feels like you're walking the same road every single day, it's time to stop and ask yourself if this direction is working. What could you do that would bring positive interruption? Maybe it's not a trip, but it's visiting new places in your neighborhood? Maybe it's time to be a tourist in your own city? It's unbelievable what happens to your dreams, your creativity, and your overall joy in life when you start to experience things that you haven't before. Sameness can feel heavy. And it can

also feel boring. I know that we don't all feel we have the resources we need to begin to live the lives we want. But before
you default to giving up, I want you to check and make sure
first that what you're craving isn't possible. When I came back
home, I made a commitment to show up in my life here the
same way I did on that trip. And do you know what? I have experiences regularly now that feel like when I was on vacation.
Trips are wonderful, I love them, but I do not want time away
from my life to breathe. We don't need to escape our lives. We
need to create lives that meet our needs. And when I feel like I
want to escape my life, it's time to stop on my path and remind
myself of my power. Remember your power.

Part 3

WHERE YOU'RE GOING

7

COMMITTED:
ON THE
COVENANTS
WE KEEP

Even a job where lateness was a crime couldn't get me out of bed on time. On active duty in the military, I still found myself rushing out the door, boots untied and everything unbuttoned, hauling ass to formation before I'd be in trouble. I was seldom late (maybe three times in five years), but I was always rushing. So you couldn't have sold me the dream that one day I would wake up and abruptly become a morning person. I was the quintessential night owl who was constantly side-eyeing how anyone could be so happy before 11 a.m. I'd see people jogging down the street while I trudged along with my dogs and genuinely couldn't understand what would motivate them other than potentially wanting to beat the heat of the afternoon. But forget the heat, I would rather run in the humidity of south Georgia at 3 p.m. (I've done it many, many times) than get up early. That was my motto. Night owl for life.

But as part of my covenant with myself to experience more joy daily (in the last chapter), I'd committed to finding ways to make time for what I love more often. I'd already had day after day and year after year of dreading the next day. During moments of depression, during moments of grief, and even when those two culprits weren't visiting, I'd felt I had too many days when I woke up not looking forward to what was coming in the morning. I wanted to change that.

I remember a time when I dreaded going to work every day. I didn't know what Sunday scaries were because I had everyday scaries. At one employer, there was always a possibility of losing your job based on the mood of the managers. Your employment was based on a scale of how well liked you were plus work output, which meant you couldn't have a life. It was just work, work, work. No passion, no fun, just paper-pushing work mixed with office political drama. I found ways to try to enjoy myself in that job, but it dulled my light.

I'd told myself that once I worked on my own, I wouldn't have to worry about those situations anymore. I'd get to do what I love, and every single day would feel like a holiday. I absolutely love working for myself today, but every day is not a holiday. I truly love what I do, and I don't have those scaries anymore. But I noticed I was still carrying many of my unhealthy habits from my previous workdays, and they were still impacting my ability to look forward to the next day. Even while working for myself, I felt like all that was ahead was still work, and even if it was something I loved coming up, it still didn't get me jumping out of bed and ready to go. I needed things to look forward to for me, so that I could bring that fullness into the rest of my day. And then this moment happened.

Prior to the morning I'm about to tell you about, I'd been selling myself the story that I was thriving in the evening, but really, I was always playing catch-up. The truth is that I wished I could be up in the morning like the folks I was side-eyeing. I knew that getting up early would give me more time back to myself. And more time meant more independence. But knowing all of this wasn't a motivator. I'm sure you've been there. Where your routine or something in your life needs to change, but you don't know how to influence yourself to make it happen.

I was skeptical, especially when it felt like the wellness world had pegged morning people as folks who'd cracked some kind of happiness code that I and so many others were struggling to believe was achievable. I had all these feelings about early rising, and yet here I was one December morning, being woken up by what I believe were my guides at 4:50 a.m. So early, the sun was still enjoying the sight of another part of the world. I didn't feel tired that first morning and I wasn't even disturbed by my being awake, which was all unusual. To my surprise, I knew exactly what I was supposed to do as I grabbed my things to go downstairs to my living room. I was going to meditate. I was moving as if this was all planned beforehand when it absolutely wasn't. I allowed my body to lead me and for once I was just following along. Now, y'all know my previous struggle with meditation and intentions. You know I moved past it, and by this morning, I'd been a meditation teacher for years. But a 4:50 a.m. meditation teacher? That wasn't me.

Have you ever found yourself doing something that "wasn't you"? You're reading more books when you felt you never had time before. You're drinking more water and you've always been a soda person. Without notice, your body tells you that it's ready for change, and you oblige. This is such a special union. To be in tune with your body enough to trust where it is leading you. To be willing to let go of any definitions of "what's you" and make space for something new to exist.

I could feel I was being called to change my practice and be alone in the kind of stillness where the world was at motionless rest. And for the first time, I wanted to answer that call. I wanted to feel that kind of calmness. Where I knew that I wasn't going to be interrupted, because if anyone should wake up and see the time on their phone, they'd roll over and go back to sleep. The "ungodly" hours, as some call them. But for the first time, I saw them as hours when I could connect straight to God, maybe because there was less interference? Not so many messages trying to get through, because most were still in the middle of their dreams on my side of the world?

After that morning, day after day, I'd sneak out of my bedroom, walk past my dogs, who would look at me like I'd lost my mind, and meditate. It was blissful. No noise-canceling headphones needed. No cars driving by. Not even the sound of birds chirping yet. I'd meditate for about twenty-five minutes, and it was so fulfilling that I could feel my cells responding. Afterward, I'd write in my journal about what I experienced or saw, and I'd just sit with myself.

It felt like a remembering. Like there was a time when I was receptive to this kind of flow before I'd committed to ignoring my alarm clock. I was being asked to come back to myself in a new way. It wasn't a demand; it was a request. I could've heard that call for meditation and decided to roll over and try to go back to sleep. I could've heard that call for a deeper form of stillness and picked up my phone and scrolled instead. But I didn't; I listened. I listened to this inner knowing, my inner knowing, and I let myself be led to my next journey. Each step on our path is a choice. It's important to remind ourselves that it's an honor to get to choose. When you feel the urge to shift, are you willing to listen?

BASE CAMP

Lalah Delia has a quote: "She remembered who she was, and the game changed." There are times when we forget what we're capable of. There are times when we remain committed to who we say we are, even when it's not who we want to be. But when you remember the breadth of what's possible for you, you might be willing to give a chance to other definitions of who you are or could be. With this shift to my mornings, that honestly was feeling a lot simpler than I'd imagined it would be; it felt like I was uncovering what always existed within me that I was finally open enough to witness and experience. Keyword: **open.** None of it was easy when I was closed off to the idea. None of it was easy when I was unable or unwilling to do the things that would help me maintain this new routine. This was a different level of commitment to myself and my journey. At the beginning of our journey, we're being asked to be open.

There's also a long list of things I'd love to change that haven't come with as much ease. With these things, I wasn't woken up at the perfect time with assistance from my guides, and I'm still struggling to figure out where the inspiration is going to come from to change them. I know what I just shared above seems a bit mystical. I'd always struggled with early rising, and then suddenly one day it was erased. The truth is, there were steps. There are always steps. If I'm honest, there hasn't been a lot of budging on the "long list of things I'd love to change" because they aren't a priority for me right now, even though I really want to change them.

Before I go through these steps, I encourage you to be honest about whether the things you've been wanting to change have been a real priority for you. Remember, you can be honest without being mean to yourself. You're not lazy, you're not behind, or any other list of harmful things that you might say to yourself. I know these are things I've said in the hope that it would get me going. But all it ever did was make me feel worse; of course it did. Who would feel ready to be brave and vulnerable enough to try something new after being torn apart? Compassionate honesty will ask you to remain curious as we go through these steps about what you want to focus on, so your energy isn't spread thin trying to change everything in your life at one time. That would be exhausting and disappointing because it probably won't happen. Starting small is powerful. So what's one small thing that you can be honest with yourself about? And be proud that you admitted it. Some of us never do.

First, I had to notice (aka be aware) and admit (aka be honest) that I was uncomfortable with the way things were, even though this was my norm. It's like wearing out a pair of sneakers. You get used to how worn in they feel, and you think that this is comfort, until you put on a new pair and quickly understand how you had no support.

I also had to be open to change. In the past I couldn't even imagine changing, so I never got past this step. But once I was open, *I made space for the magic that showed up that morning.*

I began to see these early wake-ups as a moment of connecting to pure energy. I noticed I could breathe deeper at dawn. Was there more oxygen at this hour? Were the trees working harder? My lungs were begging to move and expand, to clear deep stagnation, and with ease, what felt stuck was breathed into another plane, where it could be reused for good. I was able to experience energetic shifts that I'd been working on for a long time and that felt stuck. I released worries, old beliefs, and tears. Things that felt immovable were now floating right out of me into the ether.

Every chapter in this book touches on change because every chapter of our lives involves transformation. Whether we're dealing with loss, a new job, marriage, divorce, our children growing up, new healing tools, or learning new ways of being—it's all about change. And no matter how often we walk through change, it always feels new. We like to know where the path we're on will end. Uncertainty feels unfamiliar even though life is always unpredictable. We crave knowing the ending, even when we're at the beginning. Ultimately, I think we want to know that everything is going to be okay. Isn't it interesting that I assumed something had changed in my environment, that the trees were working overtime or that my breath was deeper because of some external factor? Nothing had changed around me. I was just still enough to notice. The only change was in me. Sometimes the change we're seeking won't come from around us; it will only need to start from within.

This new wake-up routine was asking me to retrain my mind. I was retraining my thoughts. I was retraining my nervous system. What thoughts do you believe that are hindering your evolution? It's time for you to jump off the roller-coaster ride and step back on the ground. You can choose something new. This takes time. This takes patience. This takes kindness with yourself as you learn. Amid all the chaos, remember that your feet are planted. Amid all the chaos, remember that there are roots beneath you, connecting you to your support, your lineage, and your growth. You are worthy of taking up space, and when you feel free to do this, you're grounded. Grounding means reminding your energy that you are connected to the earth. That we are here and that it's safe to exist here. In what ways do you shut down the changes that you say you want before they even have a chance to blossom? Just because you don't see buds appearing, it doesn't mean that magic isn't happening below the surface. We are rooted and grounded, but we are not stuck. We keep going.

INTENT

When we say we want something to change in our lives, like . . .

> our fitness routine
> our wake-up routine
> our relationships
> our energy
> our goals . . .

or any of our commitments, it's always helpful to dig deeper and figure out *why* we want this change in the first place. On the surface it can seem like I'm just talking about waking up earlier, and that doesn't seem like a big deal. But I have sat with clients session after session who've talked to me about their desire to change something in their world that feels so minimal but impacts their lives in such a big way. You might think I'm just talking about waking up earlier, when really I'm talking about the feeling of waking up late every day, and feeling rushed before you even start your day, and heading into work; that even if you love your work, it's overshadowed by never feeling like you have time for you because you're always behind. And even when you get home in the evening, you'll still have more to do that you didn't get to earlier. It's about making space to have time to rest and not feel overwhelmed. It's not just about waking up earlier; it's about breaking the cycle of exhaustion. A cycle that really impacted so much of my life for years.

I not only wanted to get up early, but I wanted to wake up early without anger that I was up early. I was the kind of person who could barely hold a conversation before 10 a.m. This wasn't the kind of energy that I wanted within myself or to unintentionally project onto anyone that I loved. But this is what it was like when I was "forced" to get up in the morning.

When I would say that I "wanted to be a morning person," it had nothing to do with the time of day. What I was really saying was:

- *I wanted to wake up and be with my children in the morning without fighting every bit of grogginess. I wanted*

143

to have the energy to light up when we first saw one another each day.

- Waking up early would also require me to go to bed earlier, and hopefully that would translate into better rest. I wanted to feel energized, healthy, and ready to start my day.

- I wanted to have time for myself before starting my day, and waking up early was a way to do that. I could meditate, work out, write, whatever I wanted to pour into before going into Mom or work mode. No matter how much I love my kids, starting my day depleted was heavy. I wanted to release this weight.

- I wanted to have a routine that worked for me. To go to bed earlier and get up earlier would require me to have a plan. It didn't mean that things wouldn't change when or if they needed to, but for the most part I'd have priorities that I was meeting every day that were supporting me.

Sometimes our intentions are hidden underneath the blanket statements we make, like "I wish I was a morning person." And sometimes our beliefs and desires are hidden under our resentment. A lot of the energy that we put into talking trash about someone else or hating on the joy that they have is because it's something we really want. When you find yourself doing this, ask yourself: What am I really bothered about?

Why am I *really* spending my energy talking about this person? What do I need?

I knew waking up earlier would help me be able to deal with the reality of my life. I have two kids who are up by 6:30 a.m. every day. Work responsibilities that I worked my butt off to never be late on. A desire to have a well-lived life. When was I going to work out if I didn't get up? When was I going to have time to eat a breakfast that nourished my body if I didn't get up? How was I going to get the rest I needed if I was up every night till one or two in the morning?

You may be reading this thinking, "I don't need a new wake-up routine." Maybe you thrive in that area. But you know there are parts of your life that you've been ignoring for years because you don't believe there will ever be a fix. As you walk on your journey, you conveniently never turn right down those roads because you don't think there's any point. "I'll never solve this problem, so what's the point of even getting my hopes up?" And you know what? I'm not even asking you to push yourself to go down that road. I am asking that you consider being open to the possibility of finding yourself there one day. Right when you're ready.

I'm using my wake-up routine as an example, but I want you to ask yourself:

What do you want that you know will help change your life for the better, but because of beliefs or blocks, it feels impossible to get to? Alongside the many things we go through in life is the path of us just trying to have the best life we can. When we think our "beliefs" matter more than releasing what's keeping us from getting there, we're in a cycle of stuckness. When we finally become willing to see what we can let go of that can bring us the ease we've been seeking? That's freedom. It isn't about having perfection. It's about meeting ourselves where we are. This is the other side.

PS: You're not too late. It may feel like you don't want to go down that road because there won't be anything waiting for you, but trust me. The feelings of waiting for change will be replaced by the joy of what you *still* have waiting for you. You're right on time.

When I was growing up, my grandmother would always wake up at the same time every day, with no alarm. We shared a room and bed, and so when she got up, I would hear her and feel her gently put her feet on the floor to locate her slippers. Her rising would mystify me, because I couldn't understand how she was able to do this without an alarm clock. It wasn't until I started to allow the sun to greet me in the morning that I realized the rhythm of the sky was waking her. That the light peeking through the curtains didn't have to be seen as a nagging inconvenience, but an act of service.

My grandmother had my mother in her forties, so by the time I came along my grandmother didn't have much going on daily. But whatever she did have going on, she looked forward to. Trips to the grocery store or the pharmacy, or even a walk to Downtown Brooklyn to shop around. Everything was so familiar and yet she found a way to find delight in each step. She had deep purpose. She loved being a member of her community. She loved being a grandmother and a mother. She loved waking up each day even if there was going to be a similar routine waiting for her. She found joy and gratitude in her feet hitting the floor every day. These were simple things. There is joy in relishing the simple things.

If there's one thing I learned on my journeys before this, it was that I had what it takes to create change. Take a moment right now and remind yourself that *you* have what it takes too. Yes, *you*, who it seems has quit a thousand times and still hasn't made it to where you want to be. Sometimes we quit because we're redirecting our energy, and this is a good thing! There's no need in keeping something going that isn't working. Sometimes we call it quitting when what we're really doing is starting over with a new perspective.

We must be willing to suck at things. If something isn't easy, that doesn't mean it automatically isn't for us. Everyone can't play music by ear. Everyone isn't dripping in natural athletic ability. No one is born speaking any language. We all must learn. We all must practice. We all have to decide to commit. The best of the best are set apart because they always practice the hardest. Beyoncé. Kobe. Jordan. They show up. Even when they're great, they still show up. We just need to be willing to show up.

But believe me, I know you're tired of having to start over. For me, I know when it came to trying to wake up early with some ounce of happiness, I was tired of pretending that I liked it when I really didn't. Everything in me wanted extra sleep. Everything in me wanted rest. But you know what? I wasn't *just* tired. I was worn out from the life choices I'd been making. Too much giving, too much pouring out, too much sharing, and too much of me spread thin. As I look back, I wonder: Did I really need that much rest? Or did I need that much rest because of how much I was draining myself? Did I need that much rest to put up with the life I'd built for myself?

WALK THE TALK

I kept wondering how I was finally able to hear the call from God that morning at 4:50. Why on that day was I able to quiet the nagging thoughts and beliefs enough to let my knowing lead me to where I needed to be? I wanted to know because I wanted to be able to repeat it. I wanted to continue to commit to the part of me that was willing to walk when I didn't know where I was going on my journey but knew goodness had arrived and was inviting me to follow it, as it would surely lead me to more goodness on the other side.

We talked about the journeys that arise out of nowhere that we'd never choose for ourselves. Journeys filled with pain and anguish and grief. Journeys that might have light within them but still feel like they burn out the light in us on the way. But we haven't talked about the journeys like these that we *still* would've never chosen for ourselves, and yet they euphorically expand us.

Surrendering to this new commitment was creating more abundance in my life. This surrender was teaching me about my limits. Every time I thought I'd learned as much as I could about myself, there was more for me to absorb, if I was available for it. This is why it's so important to question why you're shutting yourself down and subscribing to the idea of "being fully healed" in any area. It's great to claim our wisdom, but not in the name of missing the gifts that might be waiting for us through new lessons.

Your commitments are gifts. If you look at a map of your life, you'll see landmarked "aha moments" that brought you right where you needed to be. But if you look closely, nothing *brought* you to where you needed to be. Guess who did that work? You! You decided to commit. You decided to follow through. You decided to walk.

Yes, there are moments when "the Universe is conspiring"

on our behalf, one of my favorite "I know this by heart" quotes from the book *The Alchemist*. But the conspiracy is usually happening in conjunction with our actions, our requests, or our desires. It's a dance.

When I think about what finally helped me answer that call from within at 4:50 a.m., it was because I was tired. I was tired of the same ol'. I was tired of complaining about not being able to do what I wanted, I was tired of submitting to the idea that this was something I just couldn't get past, and I was tired of my life not reflecting the power I have to make better choices. I'd been writing about the places I could feel I was overwhelmed. It was like I was walking on my path and met by flooding on the road. I wanted to keep going, but was I willing to get wet?

But when I finally got brave enough to take a step, I learned that these waters were shallow. But you don't know how shallow they are until you're willing to take a step. It's only through the step that you learn that you're bigger than the problem. It was only through the complaining that I was finally able to talk it through. Sometimes we shut our complaining down through toxic positivity, and if we're not careful, we also shut down our truth. The nagging can turn into clarity. The clarity can help you understand what you need. And then it's time for the commitment. Without the initial commitment, we don't walk. We stay in complaining. We stay stuck. We stay stagnant. We stay tired. And we get bitter. So let me ask you: Are you *tired* enough to start opening your mouth and sharing what sucks? There is truth in those moments of sharing. Your truth is waiting for you.

LESSONS LEARNED

I no longer get up at 4:50 a.m. Over time, I realized I needed a shift, and I decided to test out different times to see what worked best. I woke at 5:15. That didn't feel right. 5:30. Still not it. Then I settled on between 5:45 and 6:15. I normally wake up before my alarm, but if I'm living life and going to sleep a little later, then I'll have moments where I'm nudged awake by a very quiet alarm. I still feel the same gratitude for listening all those months ago when I was first prompted. On the other side of this, I recognized that I'd had that nudge before. Where I was praying for a solution to something that felt overwhelming and received a "call" to try something new. I don't always answer the call, even today. But even though I didn't answer it in that moment, it waited for me. I don't know if our blessings always wait for us, but I know what we need never leaves us. It doesn't mean that we should just waste time if we know we need to do something different. But it does feel good to know that if we don't hear the call or understand the next step, it'll be there waiting for us when we're ready.

Each morning, at some point before my day has even begun, I focus on feeling grateful that I've taken time to support myself. I go to bed each night proud of myself for taking the time I need. This was the purpose that I'd been searching for in my life. Purpose in the way that I go about living my daily life. In the last chapter, I talked about the joy I found on my solo trip and how I wanted to find ways to incorporate it into my everyday life. I wasn't 100 percent sure how I'd do this fully, and honestly, I'm still learning, but this was one of the gateway life-changing moments. It wasn't flashy; it was just time with me. And this may sound too simple to even spend a whole chapter of a book on, but honestly, how many of us go to bed each night not even able to name one way that we connected to ourselves that day? How many of us are doing the big things and not being able to commit? Isn't it time that we tried the "small" stuff?

It's interesting, because remember, I told you I felt like my guides had woken me up. That they were the reason I woke up that first morning at 4:50. They helped me that day and for the next few days. But after that, the work was on me. I'd have to remain committed to ensure that I continued to give myself what I needed. I had to meet myself every day and choose what needed to be done. And this is the biggest lesson: I also have to be willing to choose what *doesn't* have to be done, so that I have time for me and all the people who matter to me!

We have to want it even when it's tough. We have to want it on days when our plans get derailed. We have to want it even when we'd rather be doing something else. Because if we don't want it, it won't happen. And I regularly ask myself how much I really want it and how it feels when I go for it. How badly do you want it?

Now, on the other side of those shallow waters, a depth that I used to be unwilling to try, I knew what it meant to rise. To walk with an intention that I'd never felt before. Now when I'm walking my dogs, and I pass the runners on the street, I smile and say good morning. Somehow we ended up on the same side of the road.

8

LIMITLESS: ON WALKING THE PATH BACK TO YOU

I sat on Kailua Beach thinking about the absolute joyful mood God must've been in when this space was created. I'd never seen anything like it. The waves crashed, delighting in bringing forward the unknown. When standing at the edge of the ocean, I welcomed the loud, crashing waves. When clouds started forming, I marveled at their beauty. If only our revisiting of past lessons was viewed in the same way as the cyclic crashing of the waves.

I thought, if I was part of a universe that could create something that looked like this, it had to mean that I was filled with the same limitless beauty too. If this repetitious, breathtaking landscape was so peaceful, perhaps the recurring lessons we visit hold peace too. It had to mean that God was in a joyful mood when I was created too. That there was nothing I couldn't do. That I was molded from the same warmth, the same salt. That I carried the same healing properties within me. That we all did.

I squatted and looked out at the ocean. Then, with my finger, I wrote in the sand *limitless* and watched as the water washed it all away. It was gentle and sometimes took multiple washes for the word to disappear. Then I'd write it again and again. No matter how many times the ocean erased the word, I was able to bring it right back. It was a small action on my part—I was just writing in the sand—and yet the tiny movements were still enough. I was enjoying this playful game that the water and I were in on. I was enjoying the simplicity of not having anywhere to go or anything to do but this. What would it be like to approach life this way? When it seemed that I was coming up against limits, to just keep insisting, through gentle writing in the sand, that we are in fact limitless?

When I think about the limits that were ingrained in me, before I was aware I had them, I think about the women I watched on TV, at school, and in my life walk a tightrope between being seen as big enough, so they weren't discarded as weak, but still small enough that they weren't seen as problematic. It was a dance I'd also mastered, and I unconsciously kept putting opportunity after romance that required me to be willing to disappear from myself.

I was regularly reminded that I was also powerful, but not in all ways. Ensuring I was independent and able to think and provide for myself was critical. I don't believe I was taught any of these limits as a way of negatively swaying my opinion; in fact, I believe it was out of protection. I was being taught about the realities of the world *as the women in my life had experienced and seen it*. I was powerful, but not *that* powerful. They wanted to prepare me for life, without a ton of surprises. They wanted me to feel equipped in ways that perhaps they had learned the "hard" way. They wanted to save me. This was limitless living for them. Getting to "free" me.

In a previous chapter, I shared a Clarissa Pinkola Estés quote about how wounds can be a door to our healing. I held many limits, and therefore, there were many doors to unpacking them. I hoped that by opening those doors, I'd find the path back to the version of myself that was infinite.

BASE CAMP

We're programmed by our families and environments without even being aware that it's happening. We absorb our surroundings, the words we hear, the wisdom that's imparted, and the mistakes our caretakers make without even noticing. This coding happens throughout our formative years, the base camp of our lives, if you will. We don't all unconsciously choose to repeat the cycles in our families, as some consciously decide to be just like their caretakers in certain ways. Others find that they want to be nothing like them. But for many of us, we look up and see that we haven't carved out a life for ourselves in the way that we believed we did. We are imitating the people we blame for our misfortunes without even realizing it.

In families you might talk about how a sibling inherited your father's eyes. Or perhaps how a cousin walks just like your aunt. Or maybe your baby comes out looking just like a grandparent and everyone can see the similarities are uncanny. We openly discuss the ways we inherit these genetic dispositions, yet we don't often discuss the programming we inherit from our families. Our work is to unlearn these inherited limitations. To walk along, trying to unweave the toxic patterns that keep showing up in our lives, even though we don't know how they got there. Perhaps it was something our parent or caretaker went through that was a formative experience for them and so they then implanted the limitation in us, often as a gift of protection. But without any context, these safety limitations frequently hold us back. Placed within us from a place of scarcity and fear, they limit our direction and constrain our path forward. *We can hold the realities of the world without allowing these challenges to become walls.* It can be upsetting to have to do work that you know isn't yours to do. But as we learn to look at our own journeys with compassion and see how we may have absorbed our surroundings without realizing it, then we can also see how our parents might've done the same. And we can hold compassion for them too.

If we hold on to the idea that we can't have love, or success, or opportunities because of what we did or didn't receive from our parents who did or didn't show up, we're limiting ourselves in the future. We're also limiting ourselves right now. It's hard to swallow that pill; trust me, I know. We talked about this earlier in the book, but it can feel validating to have someone to blame. Again, I'm not here to put a burden on you for the things that you've endured or survived in your life. What I do want you to know is that despite the ways you may have encountered circumstances that said you are small and insignificant, you are as powerful and mesmerizing as the ocean. Every tiny movement that you make toward understanding your potential is breaking those limits down.

INTENT

The days after Steve had been out binge drinking were always the worst. He'd often sleep all day and wake up just long enough to eat or smoke his Marlboros. The house would be so quiet with the TVs turned down lower than usual. I remember whispering to my grandmother as we cooked lunch, and she would whisper back. There was that much caution to ensuring he remained undisturbed. As I grew up, this routine would upset me deeply. This sense of my world having to revolve around him, her world having to revolve around him. There was never any consequence on his part, it seemed. Obviously, he missed out on a lot, and that's the nature of the life he lived. But in our home, it felt as though he was walking on air. He could do no wrong.

While journeying through the many limiting beliefs I held, I found myself circling right back to the path of forgiveness around my upbringing with Steve. This was completely unintentional as I was exploring the limitations I held about myself. But this will happen to us sometimes. We'll be exploring what we believe is a new healing journey and find ourselves back on a path we didn't intend on walking again. A path we thought we were done with.

I don't believe that I would've noticed my feelings of helplessness around being quieted after his binge-drinking episodes if I hadn't done the forgiveness work that I shared earlier. That forgiveness work had softened, prepped, and opened me to continue to release and move forward. There were still places where I was blind to how I was acting out some of those past scenarios in my adult life. I was making up for how I couldn't protect myself *then* in relationships now, and it was limiting and exhausting. People were paying the price for my past through my attempts to undo what had already happened. Before forgiveness, I was unable to see within me because all my walls were up. All I saw was anger. It was only in the softening that I could curiously explore.

I think it's important to mention again that forgiveness is a choice and it's not an easy one. It can feel burdensome. But hardened long-term anger is difficult to see clearly through, especially when trying to find ourselves. My little self was still running the show with her little fists balled up, and that wasn't serving me anymore. Choosing forgiveness gave my little self the space to rest.

Forgiveness is not a step we must take in healing. It's an option. As someone who carried a ton of anger toward those experiences, forgiving myself naturally released a lot of the heaviness I was still carrying. Forgiving myself led to empathy toward Steve. Empathy toward Steve led to forgiving him. This tension and hurt and anger that I was holding was hurting *only* me. I let go for me.

161

If you choose to let go, it's for you. If it's too hard to forgive, I see you too. We don't all feel we have the option to forgive, and that's valid too. We all get to choose. Don't let anyone force you into forgiveness. Don't let anyone force you into anger. But we can honor everyone's path and story. This is healing too.

I remember one of the first times I woke up to make brunch for my husband and me when we were just dating. I love to cook, and I enjoy making food for people. But I didn't feel adequate when I accepted help. I am embarrassed writing this, but it's true. When I accepted help in the kitchen, I didn't feel like I was being a *cringe* "good woman" if I couldn't handle it all myself. "Can I help you with anything?" he'd repeatedly ask me. "No, it'll be done in a minute." I'd rush around, cooking and cleaning, barely enjoying anything that I was doing. And that morning, when I went to make his plate, he ran to grab it and went to make it himself. I was startled but didn't say anything.

When we sat down to eat in our awkward silence, I finally said, "Why didn't you let me make your plate?" He replied, "I was uncomfortable with you not letting me help you. I could understand if you were enjoying yourself, but you looked tense." Since we were just dating at this time, we didn't go down the trauma rabbit hole during this brunch, but over the years we began to unpack where our stories were coming from. I realized that I was resentfully fixing his plate, not because of any resentment toward him, but because of what I'd absorbed watching this done repeatedly in my past. Especially on days when Steve had drank, I saw the tension as my grandmother made his plate. It always looked like a hassle, and unconsciously I was moving in the same ways even though I was happy to be making brunch for my husband. This "inherited" behavior was tied to the act of making a plate, even though the circumstances were completely different. This muscle memory was limiting me.

And for him, he'd grown up where he'd seen the man in his life supporting and helping the women around him, and as offended as I was that he wouldn't let me continue to resentfully make his plate, he was offended that I wouldn't allow him to show up. We couldn't operate from a space of abundance with these limits. But with a safe and supportive relationship, we could learn how to undo them. And we did.

This same programming was impacting the way I approached money and my career. Money is such a taboo topic to talk about, but I find that having the conversation creates so much freedom about what's possible for us and releases a lot of the shame we hold about how much money we have or don't have. I also think it's important to talk about because when I was growing up, I heard money talked about only from the perspective of lack, what we didn't have. Or the lottery. If we want to expand what's possible, we must be willing to speak.

We all have different financial goals, and we all have different things we want to do to make those goals a reality. Some of us don't ever want to stop working, and some want to retire by forty-five. Some of us want to retire in Europe and some of us want to live in some remote city of the country we were born in. Some of us want to rent for life, and some of us love the idea of owning property.

Take a moment right now and think about what your financial goals are. Write them down if you'd like!

Here's the next bit. Our financial goals are often impacted by our careers. Yes, some of us are partnered or come from families that provide more of a financial cushion, and perhaps our goals aren't impacted as much by what we do for a living. But for most of us, our short- and long-term goals are impacted by the money we make, and this can sometimes create a feeling of scarcity.

Why? Well, we feel the pressure to figure out who we want to be, what we want to do, and how we're going to make it all happen before we even fully understand who we are. Whether you work a nine-to-five or own a business, it can feel like a hard goal to meet.

We may wonder:

Do I have the energy I need to create what I desire?

In the spirit of trying to meet my goals, I would push myself to work incredibly hard and burn out. I thought burnout was part of the path to success, and I ignored my exhaustion in the name of moving forward. Working hard is part of the journey, but when I work hard out of scarcity, the feeling that it's slipping away from me, that's a different energy. Do you see the limits?

Do I know the people who can help me?

I used to be under the illusion that because of where I started I didn't know the people who could help me get to where I was going. Yes, it was true that I wasn't connected in all the ways others were, but it wasn't true that my circumstances were fixed. I still had the opportunity to meet the people I needed to. Do you see the limits here?

Do I need more experience to make this happen?

There's nothing wrong with education, but some of us get stuck in a degree/course/certification time loop, hoping that the more classes we take, the closer we get to our goals. It's one thing to be interested in learning more to be better at what you do. It's another thing to feel like you have to learn more to be the best or the smartest or the most capable. The latter has an energy of scarcity. Do you see the limits?

Am I capable of making this happen?

Do you believe that what you desire is possible for you? Do you believe that you have what it takes? Learning to believe in yourself, especially if it wasn't something you were taught growing up, can cause resistance. These "limits" may not even be yours, but you'll still have to replace them with new beliefs that make space for your dreams to exist.

And if we're basing what's possible for us on the limits we carry from our families, or where we came from, or society, we may think thoughts like:

- People like *me* don't get opportunities like *that*.
- That's great for *them*, but that will never be *me*.
- I don't have *enough time* left to get to that level.

These are not the thoughts of someone who believes they're limitless. These are the thoughts of someone who is ruled by their limits. I know that there are constructs that fortify our beliefs. Real-life experiences that have shown us that there isn't always a rainbow waiting for us at the end of our journeys. I know we can't just *poof* and drop our traumas. But does that mean that we should settle? Does that mean we shouldn't go after life, and our dreams, and our abundance with all our might?

When times would get tough, and I'd been working hard on crafting my life, and nothing I was doing seemed to be working, I'd have these moments where I'd think: Everything would be easier if I was . . .

skinnier

prettier

smarter

better educated

a harder worker (even though I've been working hard
   my whole damn life)

more charming

All the things I was taught a woman *should* be and that I believed I was not, which wasn't true.

I'd fallen hard for the capitalistic, patriarchal circle of life. I would blame myself for not "making it" in a system that wasn't necessarily created for winning. For anyone. None of this was helpful in creating a sense of abundance. But when I thought it was true, that because I was missing something I wouldn't have what I desired, it surely helped to limit me. And when these thoughts pop up today, because they still do, I have to walk myself through the guilt of still having them and the shame of what I believe I'm missing that others *appear* to have. After walking through the shame and guilt, I meet myself at the road of compassion and love. It takes time to get there, but I keep walking until I do. You can too. Our path is illuminated by our intentions. Having clarity helps us land exactly where we want to go.

WALK THE TALK

Take a moment right now and think about the times that you believed in certain limits around what was possible for you because you thought you were missing something. Are you missing anything? Or has your belief system limited what you think is possible? Remember, be kind to yourself.

Also think about when things were going well and the limits that showed up. For me, even when things were easeful, I still had old thoughts and worries. I wished I could live like some of the people I knew who'd never experienced the fear of not having enough to eat, so they didn't fret about running out of things. I wanted to feel the lightness that people who'd never been without appeared to have. There was no fear about throwing out leftovers that probably needed to go. There was no fear about a shirt ripping beyond repair. There was no fear about losing an opportunity. I still felt all those feelings, even while trying to incorporate limitless living into my life. I still felt like it could all slip right out of my hands because I knew what it felt like to never have it in my grasp in the first place. Still, having old feelings and fears about the past doesn't mean the future isn't possible. It didn't mean I was an imposter, even though I felt that sometimes. I was walking my own path. Look at where you stand right now. When those fears come up, look back and remember how far you've come.

I've learned that we can dream about a journey and speak life into that path and *still* struggle with having the courage to walk on it for ourselves. We can talk about what we desire like a distant memory, even though we haven't moved toward it yet. I didn't want my life to be like that. I didn't want to give up before I started. I don't want you to either. Just because your nervous system hasn't *yet* learned what it means to be in abundance, as defined by you, doesn't mean that we can't be taught it.

Jean-Michel Basquiat said, "It's not who you are that holds you back, it's who you think you're not." Many of our limits live here. They live in what we think is possible for us based on who we came from or where we came from. We cage ourselves into a belief system that makes it hard to create from abundance when we lock ourselves into a level of expansion based solely on what we've encountered. But to be limitless, we need to be able to believe in what we haven't witnessed. I know how exhausting, scary, and tiresome this can be. And yet we still need to be willing to allow new tides to roll in and wash away the old broken systems.

Think about the emotions or feelings that come up in you as you read about money and relationships. Do you feel excited? Do you feel uncomfortable? Are you judging me, yourself, or others?

Allow those murky feelings to direct you to where your limits live. It doesn't mean that by looking at your feelings we'll automatically change capitalism, or the patriarchy, or any of the systems that need to be erased. And knowing that is still a limit for me sometimes.

But give yourself the space to explore. Give yourself space to try. Give yourself the freedom to keep going beyond where you believed you'd reach. This is a reminder to stay focused on what you want and how you can create it, rather than focusing on what feels too far away. You can deal with what feels far away as you get closer, but right now, what about what you can reach by just putting your arms out? And if the goals you wrote down feel too far away, I understand. There are many goals that I have that seem far-fetched too.

I want you to look at previous goals that you didn't think were possible but became your reality. What did you encounter on those paths? What did you learn about yourself? Erykah Badu said, "Write it down on real paper with a real pencil. And watch shit get real." Isn't it wild what you were able to achieve that at one point felt impossible? And yet here you are doubting that you can do it again?

Being limitless is not the absence of doubt. We may still question whether things will come true. The timing still may not be when we planned it or wanted it. And yet there is so much power in not giving up. There is so much power in our walk. There is so much power in being curious about why this dream was placed within us in the first place.

It's hard to imagine the other side of a place you haven't been. When we think about the future, we think about it without any foresight. We don't even know what's happening tomorrow. It's the most vulnerable place we can be. It's the practice of childlike imagination. It's the same surrender that the ocean asks of us. To trust we'll be washed back to shore.

When I thought about the limitations I had, I could see why the patterns in my life looked the way they did. I could see why I was always trying to fit in, I could see why I was always picking the wrong partner for me, I could see why I lived in scarcity mode, and I could see, for the first time, that this didn't have to be my forever experience.

I remember, when I was an adult, finally asking my grandmother about her making Steve's plate every day. I'd always seen it as an act of service and something that she was doing to ensure he felt seen. I always wondered why she thought he deserved it. But her response . . . it's something I'll never forget. "I make his plate so that I can make sure there's enough food left for everyone else." It shocked me. This act of service wasn't solely about him or his needs as I'd assumed; it was about us. It was an act of preservation and simply a smart thing to do. I was judging her choices based on a life experience I hadn't lived. I had inherited a whole limiting belief system through observing body language as a kid that I didn't understand. This concocted story was impacting my life even though it wasn't true.

I'm learning that a lot of the stories I had as a kid were because things weren't always explained. Since I was an observer by nature, trauma had taught me to learn quick and get it right the first time. My journey to limitless thinking and living has required me to poke holes in the stories I thought were keeping me safe. My journey to limitless living has required me to be willing to look at the naive parts of me. The parts that are still growing up. That are still gaining wisdom.

What "blanket" beliefs have you been given that aren't a reflection of the path you're on in your life?

LESSONS LEARNED

When I sat on the beach that day, tracing *limitless* in the sand, it was an affirmation. This was a fact. Not an idea or something that could be true. It was real. Our journey is to remove anything that gets in the way of receiving this fact as the whole truth that it is. It wasn't just something that was true for others; it was real for me. It's also for you!

Limitless living in action would require me to show up like I believed anything was possible for me. Ask yourself these questions that I'd been too afraid to ask myself:

- What was I afraid to hope for because I didn't want to be proved wrong?
- What did I keep to myself because I thought it was ridiculous to say out loud?
- How could I honor the people who didn't believe in this for themselves, by living OUT LOUD exactly as I desire to be?

This wasn't just about manifestation. This was about embodying what I desired. I didn't have to be wealthy to be limitless. I didn't have to be a CEO to be limitless. I didn't have to be on all the "best this and that" lists or the "successful by _____ age" lists to be limitless. Status is a potential outcome of success, but *it doesn't guarantee fulfillment*. Please remember how you want to feel while choosing what you want in your life. It's not just about what the world thinks about us. It's about how we feel too.

If I'm a living embodiment of limitless living, I see opportunity ahead. I'm sure of what I bring to the table, even if you're not. I'm aware of what I want and I'm not afraid of losing when I share what I need. I'm okay with losing you if it means choosing myself. I'm okay with not having to take on people as projects or students. I'm okay with using my energy to enjoy my life, rather than believing that I'll get to do that one day when everything is perfect. Limitless living is not perfection. But it'll be perfect for you.

Don't let pessimism steal your peace. Don't let the hard times of your past rob you of the possibility in your future. Don't let your inability to figure out why people are who they are or why they've done what they did keep you from moving forward. It's time to claim something else if what you're currently doing isn't working!

Circling back to that path of forgiveness with Steve was for my soul. When we start to see these revisiting moments as gifts, the sweetness of their arrival comes quicker. Nobody wants to revisit hard times. But a part of healing is being willing to go down the roads that life is inviting us to.

There was a lot of truth to the warnings that I'd received about life. And yet, if I walked around with that energetic frequency, I'd miss out on the things I crave. Some paths are just like that beach in Kailua. While walking, I can allow the waves to wash away what I'm ready to release. I'm choosing to look at myself the way I'm sure the sky looks at the ocean. As a reflection of itself. As a reflection of its expansiveness. As a reflection of unbounded limits.

9

TRUTH:
ON HONESTY
AS OUR
HUMBLE GUIDE

I used to have a finicky relationship with telling the truth. I was taught of its importance from the perspective of lying not being what "good people" do. Many of us were taught this by parents or even in school. And I don't know about you, but my mom and grandmother had thoroughly convinced me they had "eyes in the back of their heads" so they always let me know that if I did decide to lie, they'd find out anyway, so don't do it. I remember searching both of their heads for these eyes as a little girl. Moving the hair aside and wondering how these eyes would look once I found them.

My relationship with being truthful was uncomfortable because I'd spent so much of my life lying. These weren't outright **bold** lies, but they were cover-ups. And I won't even lie to you right now and act like some of them weren't bold lies as well. This is hard to admit. Society paints liars as the worst of the worst. And yet we have *all* lied. We have all hidden something we thought would hurt someone. We've all said we were busy when we weren't. We've all said there was traffic when we were running late, when there was absolutely no traffic at all. We decide when we think a lie is vicious, when we think a lie is for the better good, or when we think a lie is necessary. These definitions vary from person to person. But no matter the rationale, it's a lie.

I would often tell what I considered to be "cover-up lies" about the truth of what was happening at home. Cover-up lies about the truth of how I felt about myself. So many cover-up lies. These lies were told from a place of protecting myself and others. I understand that not everything is everyone's business. Boundaries in all things. But when you're taught to keep so much in *through lies*, withholding can become the default option. And then you find yourself not just lying to others; you also lie to yourself. I believe this is how we begin to believe our lies, live a lie, and feel trapped by our false realities.

I've shared my experiences throughout this book, and through them I've also learned that for abuse to exist, you often can't contend with the truth. Abuse relies on lies to survive. Abuse relies on you not speaking the truth. Releasing those deeply embedded stories was part of my walk. As I continue to grow in my life, I want to live and breathe my truth. The good and the ugly. Now, and forevermore.

This journey wouldn't be one of integrity if it remained based on the old standards I had about truth. Owning what living in my truth means to me now would allow me to change my generational path. A new direction based on new principles.

When you think about your life, what has the truth meant to you? Has it been a guide, or has it felt like a shatterer of dreams? Has it been a reminder of what you feel you've lost? We're often asked to tell the truth. We're often asked to show up with integrity. We often look for people to be honest with us. But how honest are you with yourself? How willing are you to listen when someone shares the real them?

BASE CAMP

Existing within a facade may feel like a safer place to reside. We get to create a reality and project it, with no one ever knowing what's really going on. We live in a society right now that's gotten good at doing this, because with filters and social media posts, we can pretend we have a certain lifestyle or that we're someone we aren't. A lot of us like this fairy-tale land that we live in. It feels better than looking at reality. So many of us feel like our lives don't have meaning in comparison with someone else's life, when we don't really know what they may have gone through alongside building what they have. We're measuring ourselves against them without a full understanding of their experience.

I've found that so many of us also fear the truth. We fear the truth because we've seen people torn apart for choosing to live their truth out loud. We've experienced what it feels like when our truth isn't received with love, and it scares us to give that kind of power away. All of these experiences can make us weary of walking our paths with authenticity. But there is power in knowing who you are, and not wavering, no matter how strong the winds get.

It's one thing for someone to not like whomever you're projecting yourself as, but it's another thing for someone to say no to the real you. But resisting the truth is one of the things that's holding us back. Because if we're not in the know on what we really think and feel, then what are we basing any of our decisions on? If we're not admitting how we really feel, then why are we saying yes to anything that we're committed to? Who do we really think we're protecting when we hide information from ourselves or others?

Despite all the fears we may carry about living in truth, the truth is our light. It's our North Star. It's the point that we follow and with certainty know that if we keep going in its direction, we're going the right way. The truth never asks us to do anything. The truth never tries to bargain with us. In fact, the truth is so plain that if we're not careful we could walk past it, distracted by the excitement and drama of fiction.

But as I type this, I feel my ancestors' gazes. My ancestors were secret holders, expecting each family member to pick up where they left off. I knew that this was the bond we held when they were living. I now know and believe that in their current energetic form, existing in what I believe is among all the good and unbiased energy that being an ancestor offers, they wouldn't have the same desire for me. I feared letting them and everyone down by not living within the secrets. But I decided I would not carry that torch. Even in writing this book, I could feel the desire to hold back out of fear of what people may think. Am I complaining too much? Does this sound whiny? Isn't life hard for most folks in some capacity, so should I just shut up about my story? Why does any of this matter? These were the same hurtful questions that I'd ask myself throughout my life anytime discomfort showed up and I had an opportunity to speak about it. I'd question whether I had suffered enough to share. But truth is not a "who's hurting the most" contest. You don't have to have the most scars to have a voice. Here, *truth* is a verb because its definition is based on the action we take. It is a loving way of being and showing up for yourself and in the world.

When I think of speaking our truth, I think about the throat chakra, the fifth chakra in the body. While in my yoga certification course, I learned that the Sanskrit word *chakra* translates to a wheel or disk. Our energy is thought to spin in wheels through our spine and throughout our body. There are thought to be chakras that exist above the head and below the feet, but there are seven main chakras in our body.

The throat chakra is in our throat on the physical body and it's where we speak our truth. It is the space where we audibly share what feels aligned with who we are, what we desire, and even our needs. I remember when I had trouble speaking my truth, before I was even aware of my energy or knew what chakras were, I would feel my throat get tight. Sometimes it would even ache before or after trying to explain myself. Before sharing something that caused me pain, I would feel the words swell up at the base of my throat, and if I was too afraid to speak or perhaps to even allow a cry to come out of my mouth, I'd physically swallow the pain and the words and the fear all back down. Once I would do this, not only were the words gone from that moment, but they'd also disappear from me as well, inaccessible until the next time they tried to come to the surface again. My words and the emotions felt so big, I was worried I wouldn't be able to handle all that came with allowing them to be shared.

Part of healing our throat chakra is learning how to speak our words with intention. To learn to interweave our words with honesty without it landing with our people in a harmful way is an art. So many of us have only witnessed the truth used as a weapon. We've seen it thrown at unsuspecting victims with aggression and arrogance, hitting like an arrow being shot from a bow.

But our truth is a humble guide when used with love. Following our truth is how we know we're on the right path. All the paths that I curiously explored with you in the previous chapters are what lead me to my truth, and the same is true for your journey. We unweave the stories we carry and have an opportunity to hold a real fortune, our wisdom. And once uncovered, we can move forward knowing that we're walking with integrity.

INTENT

If we're running from the truth, we're also running from moving forward, whatever that may look like to you. You get to define what acceptance looks and feels like. You get to define what clarity looks and feels like. You get to define your intentions. You get to create the life you want, but if you're running from the truth, you don't know what you need because you're shielding yourself from it. Your intentions won't be able to lead you because they're blocked by dishonesty. We can see what we're walking toward if we keep going, and maybe we're not ready for it yet. Maybe we want to stay where we are in the hope that something will change about our reality, making it more palatable. But if we want to land safely and in wisdom, it's time to be real with ourselves and others.

Let's do a throat chakra exercise together. Read the following sections out loud. It can be as loud or as soft as you'd like. Be patient, take pauses, and really feel each word.

Speak

Every time I open my mouth to speak with genuine honesty, I free myself. The truth doesn't have to be sharp, even though it's not always pretty. But it does help me choose myself.

There have been times when I've had to tell people I love a truth that I knew they wouldn't want to hear. There have been times when I've had to admit the truth to myself, and wished I had another tale to tell. There have been times I've shared a truth that I mulled over for days, fearing the outcome, only to be lighter because it was now in existence. Speaking with honesty is a part of the journey. **We're for sure not healing to continue to live a lie.** But why is it so hard to say it all out loud?

One of the reasons is because once you tell the truth, you can't take it back. Once the words escape your mouth, they're cemented into the world. Yes, you can change your mind and your journey can lead you to a new version of the truth. But we can't change how what we share is received by those we tell it to. Even with this knowing, *silence is not safety.*

There is a quote that says, "The smarter you get, the less you speak." I believe that our wisdom helps us know *when* to speak and which words to say when we do. Like most things in life, this is a practice too.

Feel It

My inner knowing is part of my truth. When my gut nudges me, it's asking me, Is this what I really want? I have felt what it feels like to know when something isn't for me, and I've done

it anyway. Self-betrayal is a human experience. I'm not at fault
for not always honoring my intuition. I can choose me next
time. I can change my mind now. I am free to follow my truth.

Things may not always work out the way we hoped, but I
do believe the other side of healing our relationship to our
truth is knowing what it feels like when something is no longer working and doing something about it.

And what's even better? When we take the action and set
the boundary, or end the relationship, or start the project—
whatever it is that needs to be done—we strengthen that
feeling of "yes and no" within us. It gets stronger and stronger
until one day we feel and *understand* our knowing *before* we
give an answer. We know that the answer is no as soon as
we're asked the question or offered the opportunity. We know
that we want to do it as soon as we read the email. This is
the other side.

Memories

I am free to tell the truth about my past. I am free to tell the
truth about who I am. I am free to tell the truth about what I
want in my future. Sometimes the hard memories make it hard
to speak. I can find safe spaces to be held in my vulnerability.

Many of us like to pick and choose which parts of our stories we'd like to hold on to. Maybe you like the stories that highlight the winning parts of your personality. Maybe you cling to the stories that share the ways you were a victim and how you survived it all anyway.

We can learn a lot about the truths we adhere to by the way we tell stories about our past, the stories we choose to tell, and the ones we hope to create in our future. As we talked about earlier, the past is always a powerful place to learn more about ourselves. The past isn't necessarily who we are today, but it is part of our journey.

WALK THE TALK

I want to share a story with you about the truth by using one of my absolute favorite TV shows, *Charmed*. As I talk about the show, I'll be sharing lessons on the truth as it can relate to our real lives.

Charmed is a '90s series that takes place in San Francisco, where three sisters are living together and trying to get their careers and love lives to take off. Through a series of events, *they uncover a truth* and learn that they were born good witches who essentially help protect the balance of good in the world while eliminating evil, and from the moment they learn this, their lives are completely turned upside down.

The truth can make life feel like you just dumped it all into a blender and turned the power on. You unearth one thing and now you feel like you can never go back to who you were before you knew what you uncovered, even if you wanted to. You're not able to live or make decisions the way you were in the past. The truth can, and often does, shake things up. This is why we sometimes fear it.

Each sister has an individual gift or power that helps them do their job of fighting evil. **The more honest they are** (aka using their power for good) and the more they evolve in their new role, **the more their power grows.** One of the sisters, named Piper, starts out just being able to freeze time. But by the end of the series, she can freeze individuals, speed time up, slow it down, and the opposite of freeze, she can create fire and blow things up. **The more she learns to trust herself and trust that she's on the right path, the more her power unveils itself to her.**

Our gifts are revealed to us the more we tell the truth too. The more honest we are with ourselves, the more we can learn about what we're capable of. The more we're willing to lean into the gifts we have that can feel scary at first, the more we learn about the reason we have these gifts in the first place.

After months and months of the sisters having evil villains

show up at their home, you'd think they'd eventually become a little weary of meeting new people, right? You'd think that they would have enough evidence at this point to prove that most people they meet are trying to hurt them. There are even points during the show where I am basically screaming at the TV because I can't believe that they can't see how shady a person is whom they've decided to help. **But they continue to trust that all will be well in the end. They trust in their ability to make it through.**

Sometimes it can be hard to trust your knowing when friends or family turn out to be people you can't trust. When you've met people who don't have the same values that you do, and you believed them when they said they were being truthful, it can make it hard to believe anyone, even yourself. But don't let their choices make you hardened. Don't let your human moments or mistakes make you closed off. This only hurts you. Use your discernment and trust that whatever comes your way, you have what it takes to make it through.

One day my sister, who also watches the show, talked about an episode where an evil guy named Cole shakes the hand of the three sisters' white lighter, Leo. Leo is essentially their guardian angel. He is supposed to help heal them, keep them safe, and guide them on their path. He is supposed to see and understand things that they can't because they're human and he's an angel, on another plane. He is supposed to be their first line of defense. Essentially, he is their intuition in humanish form.

When Leo and Cole meet for the first time, they shake hands. They're both pretending to be normal guys, not an angel and a demon. Leo is pretending to be a friend of the sisters and Cole is pretending to be a lawyer. When Leo shakes Cole's hand, however, he unintentionally leaves an angelic dust on Cole's hand, and it appears to sting Cole a bit. I found it interesting that in that exchange the person trying to do harm (Cole) could feel the good person's energy and instantly know who they were, but the person who was good (Leo) couldn't initially pick up on the bad energy. Leo also couldn't feel that any of his energy had been left on Cole's hand.

Is this not how it is in real life sometimes? Where, for whatever reason, our instincts can't pick up on the person in front of us and show us who they're pretending to be. Again, we may fear that we can't trust anyone, and that the truth comes with a catch. We may believe that our knowing has led us astray because if we were truly tuned in, how did we choose them?

Note: I also think it's interesting that in this scenario both Leo and Cole were pretending to be someone they're not, aka lying (insert side-eye emoji). Leo was too busy upholding his lie to pay attention the way he would've had he not been lying. But what's also important is that not every truth is for everybody. Keeping things private is not the same as lying.

When I shared with my sister, "It sucks that Leo couldn't detect Cole's bad vibes in the same way that Cole could feel his good ones. If he did, he could've warned the sisters." And then she dropped this wisdom on me: "Maybe that's the gift of being good. You *have* to be willing to see people as good up front."

Assuming people are out to get you before you have a chance to get to know them is probably not the best use of your energy. It doesn't mean that you should let strangers you don't know into your house. It doesn't mean you should jump into long-term commitments with people you're still getting to know. Discernment is still important. But it also doesn't mean that we should prejudge based on what other people have done to harm you. That's not making decisions from truth; that's making decisions from scarcity and fear. It doesn't mean you didn't learn from past lessons if they turn out to not be *your* people. It doesn't mean you weren't street-smart. It doesn't mean anything other than you were willing to walk down the path of love and trust again, and unfortunately this time you got hurt. And when you're willing to let people in, even with boundaries and wisdom, you can still sometimes get hurt.

Obviously, we're not out here fighting evil villains like in the show *Charmed*, although life can sometimes feel that way! Whew! But what it means is that sometimes our pure intentions and following our deepest truth can still lead us on paths that feel like we went the wrong way. It can feel like there is no way that following my truth could've led me here, right? While on our paths we will interact with people who have a different idea about what truth means. Over time, we'll build our inner knowing, where we can feel the vibes and know whether they're a yes or no for us. But still, sometimes life will happen. Sometimes we'll feel the vibes aren't great for us and we'll still choose them, because we get to do what we want to do. That's part of our walk too. It's our job to learn to trust ourselves no matter what we decide. It's our job to keep going.

One of the areas in which I had to learn to trust myself again was love. Looking back on those journeys, I can see how much I was ignoring so much of my truth. I wasn't even tuning in to myself, because if I did, I would have to admit that I needed to RUN!

Have you ever been in a romantic relationship where you wouldn't look at the facts? You ignore the feeling that says "it's not a good fit" because you're so deep in the fantasy of what it could be that you can't see what it really is? I have for sure been there. I have for sure chosen partners instead of choosing myself. I have let relationships drag on after the first argument with a partner where I knew in my *gut* that this was a communication issue that couldn't be fixed. I have stayed with a partner who cheated when I *knew* I wouldn't be able to move forward. I just hoped I was wrong. *And hope and truth are not the same.*

I remember that in one particular relationship I found myself pretending to be asleep so that I could go through my partner's phone. As I sat in the dark, entering the passcode, I felt the truth hit. "Yasmine, if you feel like you have to do this, the trust is already broken. The relationship is already over." I thought that I was looking for the truth, when I already knew it. That's why I was searching for some form of validation. This was not only a waste of my energy, but it was a major boundary violation. It's draining and it's harmful.

I remember when that relationship ended, I knew that I never wanted to replicate that kind of behavior. Not only did I not want a partner whom I couldn't trust, I didn't want to be the kind of partner who violated trust. I set the foundation of what I wanted to bring into my future. I got clear with myself about what I didn't want to happen again. I got clear with myself about how I had set myself up based on hopes that weren't real.

The other side of hope is truth.

Living in truth doesn't mean the absence of hope, though. It just means deciding that you're going to stay committed to something or someone based on what's real, not on what you wish it could be. The truth can be heartbreaking. It can smash dreams. It can cause us to change course. We may end up in places we never imagined we'd be.

There have been many instances in my life when the truth has smacked me so hard across the face I forgot where I was. But those moments happened only when I refused to listen and be honest the first, second, and hundredth time. When I stubbornly ignored what was right in front of me, the truth would be forced to get indignant.

When it came to those unhealthy romantic relationships, I had to admit to myself that I was allowing partners to disrespect me in the name of what I thought was love. The truth was that I had never seen healthy love, nor had I examined what healthy love looked like for me. I was in relationships with no clear boundaries, and this was leading to recurring themes that didn't stop just because the partner changed. I was getting the bare minimum and I was unwilling to be honest with myself about that.

LESSONS LEARNED

As you think about where you're headed in your life, what do you know you don't want to bring with you? What do you know that you're ready to leave behind?

In a quote from the book *The Invitation* by Oriah Mountain Dreamer, she shares, "It doesn't interest me if the story you are telling me is true. I want to know if you can disappoint another to be true to yourself; if you can bear the accusation of betrayal and not betray your own soul, if you can be faithless and therefore trustworthy."

The truth will feel like deception sometimes. We may be shocked to hear that people feel differently about us than we thought they did. We may reveal things about ourselves that others find hard to hold. That's the thing about the truth. Everyone is wondering if the recipient can really hold it. Can they witness who I am and still hold me with love and tenderness? Can they witness who I am and not judge me? Can they witness who I am and still honor my journey? Can they hear my stories and still want me around?

What do we do when they don't choose us? When we're walking our path with honesty, and they don't like it? Ask yourself, How often am I willing to start over, even when it means walking the road by myself? Here's the thing: people who love you will be cheering for you when you decide that your truth is the only thing that matters. The people who are jeering at you when you make decisions based on your integrity? They need you to stay in the dark to be able to keep up their games.

For me, this journey has been one of choosing to be who I am, even when I question it. Unapologetic living is intense, y'all! It's not about telling everyone what you think about them. Unapologetic living asks *you* to be honest with yourself about how you're showing up. Looking at yourself in the mirror is the real work.

EPILOGUE:

FREEDOM

We know that the grass isn't always greener on the other side, yet that doesn't keep us from wondering what's going on over there. We peek our heads over the proverbial fence with fascination about what could exist. Just the desire to look is a pull. It tugs on our imaginative strings and curates a world where what we desire exists for real, not just within us.

I went on a hiking trip for my thirty-sixth birthday, and two years prior to this trip, I had hurt my knee. It was the kind of injury where you feel the pop and you stop right in your tracks. Having never had an injury before, I thought I would ice it and that everything would be fine in a few days. But this injury required X-rays, many physical therapy visits, and years of full commitment to build strength again. There would be times when this injury would flare up and I wasn't able to walk. I'd have to cancel plans, or figure out how I was going to carry things when traveling. My freedom felt completely limited. I didn't think I'd be able to have the independence I had before.

Freedom is valuable. Freedom is in choice. Freedom is powerful. Freedom is often what we're seeking when we start walking a new path. We want to find an open road, where we aren't constricted by fences and property lines and barriers. We don't want to have to tippy toe and sneak a peek. We want paths that take us through open roads and vast views. We want hills and hidden lakes. We want wildlife that roams free with ease. We want to breathe deeply.

Because this hiking trip would be four days of mountainous hiking, four hours a day, I knew I'd have to really prepare. I started working toward the trip six months out, walking for hours every day. I started strength training again, despite the thoughts I had that I wasn't strong enough to do it. And to my surprise, I completed each hike, and I loved it. In fact, it's turned into one of my favorite hobbies. Although I was able to walk before going on the hiking trip, and I could already sense how I'd become stronger, I didn't see it in real time until

I was hiking. Mostly because, while training, I would never push myself because I was afraid to reinjure my knee. That's the thing about being wounded. You know what it feels like, you know how hard it is to get over it, and you'll do almost anything to avoid it. But it's only through trying again that we know we can withstand the weight. And while hiking, I felt that sense of freedom that I thought I'd lost. A sense of freedom I'd probably have had for some time if I'd not been so afraid to try.

There will be times when life will feel constrained. Much like I felt when I was injured, we won't feel like we can walk our paths with the same power. But there is always freedom on the other side of hardship. Freedom in discovering your resilience. Freedom in unearthing your truth. And the freedom to decide to do what feels impossible. This is the other side. Where we learn that the hard walks give us the freedom to access what we want. We're not on these paths to be punished. And if we're honest, some of these paths are ones we're on because we're not minding our business. But most of our paths are just life. Among them are the values we learn once we arrive. Arriving is not the end, but it is a new beginning.

When you think about arriving at the other side of situations that have felt tough in your life, what do you imagine will be waiting there for you? What do you feel that you aren't able to access now that you'll have once you make it there?

On the other side, we learn the value of:

Rest

Rest is where God prepares you in your dreams. The universe conspires with your subconscious and gives you signs and wisdom, ensuring that you wake up with memory of what took place. You awaken, searching for the meaning of the dream, but the encoding is already on your spirit.

Remind yourself that rest is where you can lay down your concerns. You won't always awaken with answers. But resting is an affirmation that you trust that things will be okay.

Pleasure

I refuse to spend my life only walking paths that teach me through pain and trauma. Learning to allow love in and receive care will be one of the greatest teachers of your life. Ask yourself what love has allowed you to witness in yourself as well.

Never Giving Up

It's only through completing a path where you literally want to quit every single moment that you learn the power of not giving up. There are moments in life when we need to quit things that have been over for some time. There are moments in life when we are holding on to things that aren't providing anything other than weight.

And then there are moments when we need to keep putting one foot in front of the other because what's waiting for us will outweigh the struggle. This was true of my knee injury. And this is surely true in life. I've witnessed this during all my moments of starting again. It was tough in the moment, but on the other side of divorce, or finding love again, or starting a new career, the struggles on the way were nothing compared to the reward.

Think of three paths in your life that changed you for the better. What did you learn about yourself? Why did they change you? What from those experiences do you still hold on to today?

One of my favorite parts of revisiting the journeys I've shared in this book is remembering how far I've come. I've tried as I've grown to not care about what other people think, but I think I've come to understand and accept that I *do* care. I always will. Caring deeply is part of my toolbox. And this softened part of me ensures that I'm not only highly sensitive to the potential of pain, but that I'm also highly aware of the magic that life offers as well. Caring doesn't stop me from doing me, though. And it shouldn't stop you either.

On the other side of journeys that I was sure at the time I couldn't get through on my own, I now stand with a sense of belief in myself that keeps me from walking on paths in disguise. I want to be fully seen. I want the light shining down on me. I'm no longer holding on to fears of what other people may unearth about me when thinking about the mistakes I've made or the journeys that failed. In many of these shared stories, I knew the outcome may not be in my favor. But I loved hard, and I hoped that things would work out. We all have moments when we realize that we chose wrongly because we loved others. Now I get to choose like I love me too. And so do you.

This book has probably reminded you of the journeys you've traveled, the old paths, guides, and stopping points you've seen. You've probably thought about the base camps you've visited, the intentions you set, the times you walked with no clear direction, and the lessons you've learned along the way. These stories, no matter what you've been through, are reminders that you are lovable. That you can receive. That you are light. That peace is yours. You can use these guideposts to look at where you've been and work through those stories with a therapist or friend. You can use them to help you see where you are in a current experience in your life. Or you can use them to plan the most beautiful future.

There is freedom in telling your story; start with telling it to yourself. When I decided to stop hiding in the shadows of what I'd been through and embrace the hills and rugged terrain of my life, I saw who I really was and loved her. Embracing who you are may still come with fear. Fearlessness is not where the other side resides. It's being who you are *despite* what may come that's evidence of our arrival. This is the goal.

Write notes to yourself that remind you to keep going. You don't have to be in a place where everything is perfect to write these. When you write during tough moments, you'll learn lessons. When you write during great moments, you'll affirm your journeys. Each moment matters.

Journal Prompts

Base Camp

Write out three different occasions when you arrived at a journey that you felt you'd never been on before.

These "beginner" journeys are powerful because they usually come with a lot of growth edges that teach us.

Intent

Using those stories above, can you see what your intent was on each journey?

What do you think your intent should've been looking back?

Understanding your intent on your journeys will help you learn how to focus (or refocus) on what's important.

Walk the Talk

Continuing with the stories above, when did you notice that you began to take action in each story? You didn't have to make any major changes; it could've been changing the way you think or implementing a new healing tool to ground you.

But deciding to move is a powerful moment and there are usually pivotal steps that took place before and after each situation that are important to remember.

Looking at the stories above, were there any moments when you had to circle back to a path that you thought you'd completed?

Learning lessons repetitively can be hard. But when we learn to see these moments for the gifts that they are, we can integrate this new wisdom and gain more clarity than we originally had when we first walked the path!

Lessons Learned

Write down some of the *key* moments from those stories above that put you on the path you're on right now.

What are the lessons that you learned on your journey? What are the lessons that you're still learning?

Where You've Been Check-In:

- In what ways has grief stretched you?
- Take a moment and define what thriving looks like in your life. What would a thriving you be doing? Whom would a thriving you be spending time with?
- Are you able to see how life wants you to win? If not, what feels like it's still in the way of you holding this truth?
- What were your personal takeaways from this section?
- How are you walking through forgiveness of others or yourself now?
- What from this section would you like to bring with you?
- What are you now ready to leave behind because it no longer needs to be carried?

Where You Are Check-In:

- How do you feel about today? Not yesterday, not tomorrow, right now.
- How are you learning to create joy in your life regularly?

- Is anything missing? Is there anything you can do to add it?
- Do you need what you feel is missing? Check in again.
- How are you currently reaping the benefits of the paths you've walked in the past?
- What does presence mean to you?

Where You're Going Check-In:

- What are you looking forward to that you've finally said yes to?
- What's something that's not coming with you on your next path? This can be an emotion, a story, or a belief.
- In what ways will you be winning in the future?
- What lessons are you glad you've learned for the future?
- Write an email to future you. Let future you know how you need to show up for you. Let future you know how powerful and magnificent you are. Schedule the email for a future date that you're looking forward to.
- Write a letter from future you to past you. What does past you need to know that you've never been able to say until now?

Affirmations for the Road Ahead

- I'm learning that I get to define what progress means to me. Comparing myself to others is holding me back.
- I'm learning to trust my knowing. With each experience that I go through, I learn to listen to myself with care. I learn to listen to myself like I know what I know.
- I'm learning that other people can't always give me the clarity that I'll gain by experiencing life on my own.
- I'm learning to breathe deeply when times get tough. I used to hold my breath, always awaiting the next tragedy. Now I walk with peace, knowing I have what I need to survive and be alive in joy.
- I'm learning to let good things come to me without fear. This is new, but this is my birthright.
- I'm learning to trust my instincts. If I had what I needed to survive, then I also have what I need to flourish.
- I'm learning that keeping secrets is too heavy for my soul. My freedom is dependent on my voice. Speaking my truth is opening me up for love.
- I'm learning that I could be walking right here on Earth, or I could be walking on the moon and yet I still

have the power to be on solid ground. The grounding
is within me.

- I'm learning that my energy can be influenced by other
people, and yet, I'm still in charge. I get to decide
where my attention goes.

- I'm learning that survival mode is not the only place
that I can shine. There is peace in my ability to relax
into the unknown without having to fight with each
step that I take.

- I'm learning to lean fully into the joy of good times. I
don't know when bumpy roads will arrive, and I'm not
wasting my time looking for them either. If they come,
I'm ready, but in the meantime, I choose to thrive.

- I'm learning that my peace is immovable. There are
those who believe that they can sway me, but I don't
have to walk down that path with them. When I stay
focused on where I'm headed, I don't have an interest
in meeting them where they are. This is freedom too.

- I'm learning that I don't have to have a reason to
experience joy. Being alive in this moment is reason
enough.

- I'm learning that doing things by myself is not the
same as being alone. There's nothing wrong with
enjoying my own company and living my dreams on
my own sometimes.

- I'm learning that it's up to me to change the limits that I place on my joy.

- I'm learning to ask for what I need in my relationships. Ninety-nine percent of the time, especially with my root friends, what I think is going to be a big deal is met with love and understanding. The story that I have that my needs (or any asks) are too much is just not true. This is healing too.

- I'm learning that adult friendships take work and to be honest about how much capacity I have for that work so my friends and I can show up with what we truly have. It's not always the way we want it to be, but it's honest, and that's the most loving thing we can do.

- I've learned I'm worthy, no matter who is present in my life. I'd placed a lot of expectations on my external relationships, and in many ways, I wanted them to fill the gaps. Gaps that were mine to fill. That's no one's work but mine. And also, having people in my life who care about me is the minimum. I'm no longer chasing scraps.

- I'm learning to trust the dreams that are within me. They were placed there for a reason. I'm willing to allow them to unfold. I'm willing to trust that I have what it takes.

- I'm learning that I'm a reflection of the beauty that

I see in the world. I'm not just witnessing the beauty around me, I'm part of it.

- I'm learning to acknowledge the limits that I believe and choose a different way of thinking to get me to where I want to be. I'm not too late. I'm not broken. I didn't mess up. I'm not a problem. I'm me. I'm human. I'm growing. This is healing.

- I'm learning that truth is where my power lies. When I'm willing to admit what I'm feeling, that's where my confidence lives.

- I'm learning that the truth is always within me. Anytime I think I'm being nice by hiding the truth, I'm draining myself.

- I'm learning that the truth is a gift. It gives me the opportunity to be seen by the people I love, and it also gives me an opportunity to understand the people I love on a deeper level. This is healing too.

Remember, freedom lies in remembering who you are. When you forget, come back here, and remember that you are allowed to be well. It doesn't always have to be hard.

Meditation

Here, you can find meditation resources to support you on your walk. You can listen to these meditations while sitting or lying down. The important thing is to find a position that's comfortable for you. Remember, meditation is not the removal of all thoughts and feelings. It's becoming still enough to connect to ourselves and all that is present for us to witness in our mind, body, and soul.

ACKNOWLEDGMENTS

To write any book feels like an absolute gift. To have written my second book is beyond my wildest dreams.

Thank you to my husband and daughters for your support, joy, and laughter throughout this process. Writing can be isolating, but you all kept me afloat through fun and love.

Thank you to my family for supporting me through the telling of my story.

Thank you to my team. For all the meetings, texts, and support. I'm so grateful.

And thank you to my community for continuing to support my work and being so kind along the way. Y'all are the best.